Praise for *A Dragon*

"Brown and Fuller's book fc ⟨barcode MW00478532⟩ ۱ed function within any busi.... ....ı. ı.....s on recurring revenue from an existing client base. Imminently readable, their book uses real-life anecdotes to illustrate an overarching framework for client management while supplying practical everyday advice. Whether you want to know how to say "No" to a client, or how to handle a thorny client-entertainment situation, Brown and Fuller address it. I'd recommend it for those new to client management, but those who have lived through a career of managing clients (and have the scars to prove it) might also pick up some useful ideas."

   – Chris Millner, Financial Technology Executive and Consultant

"Brown and Fuller have deep expertise in account management and bring that to bear in this entertaining book. It is light-hearted but full of useful insights, practical advice, and great stories and examples. I recommend it for anyone who regularly manages business clients, whether they are experienced or just starting out."

   – Amanda Setili, President, Setili & Associates and author, *Fearless Growth* and *The Agility Advantage*

"John and Fred have done a remarkable job of providing useful and comprehensive advice for anyone serving clients. They offer meaningful real-life examples of how to handle virtually any situation that can arise when dealing with client matters, showing that skillful client management is both an art and a science. I wish I'd had a resource like this when I was a relationship manager!"

   – Jeff Weikert, Chief Strategy Officer, Abe AI

"I've been in the client management hot seat, and I've helped to design and execute training for sales and client management professionals across my career, and for the first time there is a book that provides the critical foundations to confidently enter into client meetings and be prepared to handle its many complexities. It doesn't matter if you are new to the client management profession or a seasoned professional, this book contains all the tips and tactical how-tos to be prepared for the unpredictable and provide success for you and your client. It should be a part of any organization's client management onboarding or training program."

- Darren McAdams, VP, Strategy, Technology, Operations, a global media content & technology company

"Having done client management at the individual and executive level for the better part of a decade, this is a must-read for new client managers, and a great tune-up for those of us who have been doing this for a while! Unlike the average business book that crams 50 pages of content into a 400-page, 27-step 'simple' process, A Dragon Walks into a Meeting centers on three jobs and is something you can breeze through in a night or two. Better yet, the easy writing style and subtle humor actually make this one of the few enjoyable business books I've read."

- Brandon Horne, GM, Head of Partnerships & SaaS, Greenlight Financial Technology

"John and Fred are expert client managers, having worked with the most complex and demanding customers while at growing tech companies. This book is full of practical advice and implementable tactics for both those new to client management and seasoned veterans."

- Jim Morgan, Chief Financial Officer, CallRail

"This is a great read for anyone interested in how to engage clients and how to ensure they are looking at their client relationships with a client-first mentality."

- Melissa Jankowski, SVP, Global Strategy and Innovation, FIS

"Having managed many account teams, I can tell you that Fred and John deliver fantastic advice that any practicing account manager can implement today. They cover the topic well and deliver it with humor and great real-world stories."

- Craig Potts, Former CEO, Assurance Software

"With *A Dragon Walks into a Meeting*, Fred and John have created a highly readable guide for those new to the field of account management. If you're looking to learn more about this important part of running a business (or are an experienced account manager looking for new tricks), I highly recommend this book."

— Jardon Bouska, Chief Operations Officer, Safe-Guard Products International, LLC.

"The authors distill their years of front-line experience managing clients into what is an essential resource for anyone new to account management. Written in a highly accessible style, it offers practical, simple-to-follow advice for navigating even the most challenging client situations."

— Rob Shields, CEO/Founder Acadia Shutters, Inc.

"John and Fred are among the best in the business in managing and growing client relationships. I have personally witnessed them handle some of the most challenging client situations and relationships with the strategies and tactics they outline in this book. This is not only a must-read for people who are client facing, but also anyone who is interested in forming and maintaining any professional relationship."

— Joe Schab, COO, Leasequery

"John Brown knows client management. He was my first 'teacher' and literally is the reason I got into the profession that has driven my career. I can recall going through many of these situations with John first-hand. Having the principles documented in this book will be an excellent learning tool for new client executives as well as a good reminder for experienced professionals."

— Barry Danz, Account Management Senior Executive

"John and Fred know how to keep calm and carry on, even when the client is dropping bombs and breathing fire."

— Lynne Laube, CEO & Co-Founder, Cardlytics

A Dragon Walks into a Meeting

A Tactical Guide to Client Management

by John Brown & Fred Fuller

Published by How2Conquer
1990 Hosea L. Williams Drive NE
Atlanta, Georgia 30317
www.how2conquer.com

© 2020 by John Brown and Fred Fuller

All rights reserved. This book or any portion thereof may not be reproduced or used in any manner whatsoever without the express written permission of the author except for the use of brief quotations in a book review.

First edition, August 2020

Illustrations and cover design by Kelly Giardino
Book interior design by Emily Owens
Edited by Katherine Guntner

Printed in the United States of America

Library of Congress Control Number: 2020938946

Print ISBN 978-1-945783-07-4
Ebook ISBN 978-1-945783-08-1

Contents

Introduction...1

   Why Do We Need Another Business Book?.....................1

The Basics..4

   Customer, Client, or Account?...4

   Everyone is Client Facing!...6

   Clients as Partners..7

   You Have Three Jobs...9

   The Principles of Client Management 11

Job #1: Build and Maintain the Client
Relationship 17

   Chapter 1: We Have Relationships with People,
   Not Entities...19

      Your Relationship with Your Client is Like a Bank Account..20

      Make Account Deposits...21

      Manage Withdrawals...23

   Chapter 2: Create Connections and Seek to
   Understand..27

      Every Interaction Matters...28

      Learn Your Client..29

      The First Five Minutes..33

      Business Etiquette is About More Than Forks.............35

      Interacting with Senior Executives...............................40

      Social Media and Client Management...........................42

   Chapter 3: When It Gets Negative, Start by
   Assuming All Sides Have the Best Intentions...........45

      Remember You're Jousting with the Dragon...............46

      Take Greater Ownership...49

      Get to the Root Cause..50

      Don't Just Say No..52

      Slow Roll the No..54

Persevere Until You Prevail, or Have One More Meeting 54
Manage Your Own Thinking 55
Admit Mistakes Quickly 57
Avoid Micro-Communication Mistakes 58
Reframe the Discussion 61
Show Enthusiasm When You Do Agree 62

Job #2: Build Success for Your Company 65

Chapter 4: Think About Growth 67

Consider Types of Growth Beyond Revenue 68
Project Management 69
Goal Setting 70
Map the Organization 71
Leverage Technology 72

Chapter 5: Say Yes 77

Make the Commitment 77
Negotiations 79

Chapter 6: Remind the Client Why You are There 82

Reinforce the Value Proposition 82
Conduct a Periodic Business Review 83
Be the Master of Your Products and Services 86
The Power of Story 87

Chapter 7: Lead by Example 90

Bring Order from Chaos 90
Know Your Numbers 91
Set Up Recurring Routines 92
Manage the Executive Team 95
Leadership Beyond the Executive Team 98
Lead Operators with Respect, but Not Reverence 99
Lead Even When You Don't Know What You're Doing 101

Job #3: Manage Tasks and Demands That Get in the Way 103

Chapter 8: Business Travel 105

The Three Commandments of Business Travel 105
Dress Code 109

Chapter 9: Meetings and Agendas 112

Prepare, Prepare, Prepare 112
Avoid Technology Failures 114
Be Present, Have Presence 116
Video Conferencing 118
After the Meeting 119

Chapter 10: The Tricky Art of Client Entertainment 122

The Rules 122
Can I Entertain the Client Even If We Are Remote? 125
A Word About Expense Management 126
What If the Fun Never Ends? 126
The Dangers of Drinks 127
Harassment and Sticky Situations 128

Chapter 11: Communicate 133

When in Doubt, Communicate 134
Email as Business Communication 134
Email as Danger 140
When to Go Face-to-Face (or Ear-to-Ear) 141
Know Your Audience 143
Listening vs. Talking 145

Wrap Up & Resources 149

Wrap Up 151

Be More than a Pass-Through 151
Be a Student of the Game 151
Final Thought: A Word About Character 153

Resources...155

Further Study 155
Tools and Software...156
Example Account Review..157

About the Authors..158

Introduction

The client meeting was drawing to a successful conclusion. We had finished walking through the performance of the product and the next steps of our development roadmap. Satisfied with our outstanding performance, the client manager asked, "Any other questions or concerns?"

Mitch, our main contact for the client, slowly unfolded his arms and said, "Yeah, I have one concern." And that's when the dragon showed up. He slammed his hands on the table and exclaimed, "This sucks! You guys haven't delivered anything – your product has none of the content you said it would. I can't believe I bought into this."

Fortunately, we had several experienced folks in the room who leaned in and embraced the conversation. Mitch continued on for a few more minutes, spittle flying.

Prior to the meeting, we'd prepared – extensively – with a beautiful, fact-filled slide deck. We did all the "right" things (we thought), and yet the client meeting crashed in a wave of emotion. We were worried that the client would never buy from us again (as the best-case scenario), or worse yet, fire us. We each left asking ourselves, "Why did I ever take this job?"

One of the meeting participants was a younger client manager who was experiencing this level of tension for the first time. He would later confide that he had to fight the urge to dive under the table. This is a nightmare scenario for anyone managing clients. For some reason, they never covered this in business school. Which is the reason we wrote this book.

Why Do We Need Another Business Book?

Mastering the craft of managing clients takes time and discipline. This book is about that discipline.

We've found client management is almost nonexistent as a business topic – whether in business school curriculum, books, or training. For some reason, one of the most people- and resource-intensive activities for any organization is underserved. It could be because "hunting" (sales) is considered a hard-hitting topic worthy of discussion, but "farming" (client management) is seen as somehow easier and unworthy of much exploration. Of course, nothing could be further from the truth, and client management might even be more difficult because no one discusses how to do it the right way.

Our objective with this book is to give you the tools you need to manage challenging client scenarios. We'll focus on techniques you can execute today, not grand strategies that sound great but are unattainable in practice. We believe anyone can develop the skills to be a capable client manager.

How the book is structured

In each chapter, we'll review some basic techniques to help you grow. Each of these techniques is worthy of much more than we have here. Our intent is to outline the skills you need for basic proficiency, with mastery to be achieved as you learn. We'll do this by giving you a tactical "to do" that you can execute tomorrow with your clients and continue working on until you become an expert in each skill area. Learning by doing, even if you do not yet know it all, is a great way to get started and develop practical experience – all without attending a dreadful two-week seminar where most of your notes will gather dust on a shelf!

What if I'm an introvert?

Some of the best, most beloved client managers we have encountered are absolute introverts from technical and operational backgrounds, the kind of people who love nothing more than being alone with a good book or writing some code. However, they follow the principles of this book in a rigorous, organized fashion and are successful for it.

What if I'm coming from a different field?

We believe the universal principles we present here are timeless and apply across many client management scenarios. Regardless of your title for your role, we hope you can apply some of these lessons to your daily challenges. Even if your role does not include the management of external clients, there are many strategies contained here that are applicable to your day-to-day relationships.

Perhaps you were in your company's operations team and were recently promoted to a new role in client management. Or maybe you were in sales but are now tasked with leading a new client management team whose mandate is to grow existing clients. Or you're in a back office function like accounting or HR but have a new client portfolio you need to manage to be considered successful. If that sounds like your challenge, then this book is for you. There might even be something in here for the old pros – we can all use a refresher from time to time!

Why a dragon?

Mystical and wise, yet dark and aggressive, flout-abouts that inspire and intimidate, dragons are creatures of great intrigue the world over. Their lore has survived for millennia, but how you feel about them probably depends on where you grew up.

As a general notion, European cultures view dragons as fire-breathing, wicked guardians of gold. Asian cultures conversely revere dragons as spiritual, magical creatures. For the purposes of this book, we intend to represent neither.

To us the dragon is unpredictable, a volatile alter ego that, at times, cannot be controlled. Imagine the dragon who incinerates the room with his breath-of-rage while seemingly thinking he has it under control – that dragon. The dragon who goes from frost to inferno over an ill-interpreted word – that dragon.

Everyone reading this will one day work with that dragon, if you haven't already. In fact, the harsh reality is that most of us will at some point be that dragon. The dragon is often oblivious to his power and wields it unknowingly. It is not our belief that dragons are inherently bad but most certainly unpredictable, and the closer one gets to the dragon's gold, the greater the unpredictability.

As a client manager who is being paid by the client, you are always precariously close to the gold. It is with great forethought that we introduce the imagery of the client as a dragon, not because of a general negative connotation, but because of the role power they have, their ability to escalate quickly, and because as a client manager, you should always be on your toes.

Let our hard-won experience help drive your success

We have extensive experience in managing accounts and as client managers with several organizations, mostly technology companies. All of the tactics included here are lessons learned that, applied correctly, will achieve tangible, real-world results. Although you might be in a slightly different industry, we believe these practices will be useful in a variety of fields. Everything here is direct from the trenches, not secondhand study.

Consider this book your field guide for the practical client manager – what you can do today or tomorrow to drive success with your clients! We invite you to join us as we explore what happens when a dragon walks into a meeting.

The Basics

The work we're talking about in this book is often called "client management," so we'll default to that term, but it's also often called "relationship management," "account management," or the newest term, "customer success." Specialty roles within this type of work can be called "Key Account Manager (KAM)" or "Enterprise Client Partner." Very fancy!

Regardless of the terminology or the exact boundaries of the role, they share a common characteristic of building and maintaining trust with another organization, and the only way to do that is through building relationships with individuals.

We hear all these terms used, sometimes interchangeably, sometimes as separate ideas within an organization. In this book, we'll refer to the practice and science of "client management" as the business or function of managing clients in a pre-existing relationship – generally in a business-to-business context. In other words, the client is "sold," the product is implemented or delivered (or will soon be), and you are responsible for the ongoing day-to-day management of the client.

Customer, Client, or Account?

All businesses classify their clients with different labels: buyer, customer, client, account, key account, strategic account, relationship. The taxonomy is irrelevant, but for consistency we'll typically use "client" when referring to the customer. The typical definition of a client is a party who receives or consumes products (goods or services) and has the ability to choose between different products and suppliers.

We would amend that definition to include:

"A party who receives products from your organization and with whom an effective relationship is critical to your short-term and long-term success."

See what we did there? One, a client may or may not have the ability to choose between different suppliers, and two, the business relationship is critical to your short-term (i.e., immediate future) and long-term (forever) success. We make this distinction for a few important reasons.

Often, some of the most difficult or challenging relationships can be those where no choice is possible. We once worked on a consulting project with Company A, a large international oil-and-gas producer. They produced a chemical component as raw input to Company B, a raw materials manufacturer. The chemical component was only produced in the United States at one factory. This would seem to be an ideal relationship for Company A, with a natural monopoly that commanded high prices. Not surprisingly, Company B was less than excited about the relationship and bitter about any flaw in service delivery, no matter how minor. The two client managers for Company A had little relationship leverage with their client, and every issue escalated to the head of the Company A business unit. At the end of the project, we learned a large Asian chemical company was contemplating building a factory for the same raw material in the U.S. This could have been a business disaster for Company A, but it could also be prevented or mitigated with proactive, process-based client management.

All competitive advantages are temporary. External forces will change, but your ownership of the relationship will not. Furthermore, if a relationship is poor enough, it is not uncommon for a company to abandon the relationship in pursuit of their own solution. A client will go through a well-managed process to make the decision to dump you as a vendor – with analysis, spreadsheets, and slide presentations given to management. All of that activity is a thin veneer to disguise the fact that they are frustrated with the relationship, and the decision is solely based on how they were treated when there was no choice. Research shows most business decisions are made with emotions, not facts and logic.[1]

---

[1] See the **Resources** section for further reading on how emotions drive most business decisions.

Manage every client as though there are ten competitors lined up at the door!

The idea that a happy customer is important to long- and short-term success is not a new one, but this book is more concerned with clients beyond everyday customers that pay for our services or products. For example, we once worked in a business that was a two-sided network for electronic payments. On one side of the network were banks, who paid for the service, and on the other billers like the phone company, who received payments. Most of the economics of the service were driven by banks, with very little from the billers. Regardless, we treated the billers as clients because without them the network would not exist. They were essential to our long-term success. Some companies take this concept even further and manage suppliers almost like a client, particularly when the supplier is a critical path to daily manufacturing (such as automotive). Ultimately, this book is about managing any ongoing business-to-business (B2B) relationship.

Everyone is Client Facing!

If you broaden your definition of a client, you might start to think about your role differently, particularly if you are in a role usually considered back office. Finance, accounting, marketing, HR, and IT all certainly feel like internally facing functions, but all of these roles have a client as well. If asked, most of these functions would say their client is the company's executive team. Although this might be true, it is usually an incomplete answer. Or sometimes the answer might be something even more vague like "our customers" or "our shareholders."

Think more specifically about who your client might be. If you are in operations, it is likely your real client is the sales or account team. If you are in finance, your client might be business unit managers. For HR, it could be the company's managers.

Many times this requires admitting the painful truth that a peer at your office is actually your client. Often, your client is the person in the organization that causes you the most angst. We know a female senior executive who believes that everyone in a large company has a "Lex Luthor" – someone who is their nemesis. It may be worth considering that your "Lex Luthor" might actually be your customer – something to think about as we walk through the secrets of successful client management! (But steer clear of thinking of your client as an enemy. Such thinking will seep through and become obvious to your customer. More on that later.)

Clients as Partners

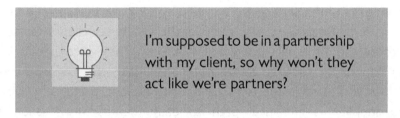

I'm supposed to be in a partnership with my client, so why won't they act like we're partners?

A recent common business trend is to refer to clients as "partners." Sometimes this even extends as far as the terminology in the contract, with "partnership" or "joint marketing" language throughout. Of course, the client manager is upset and confused because the client never acts like a partner.

We adhere to the old-fashioned notion that if someone is paying you to do something, they are a client, a customer, a buyer, or whatever you would like to call them – but most definitely not a partner. A partner is someone with equal power in a relationship. The number of people on the client side who view the relationship as a partnership is also vanishingly small. In fact, in our relationships with vendors, we do not view them as partners. We treat them with respect, and never let emotions drive the conversation... but they are not our partners.

The vernacular of "partnership" can be misleading and will change with the temperature of the relationship.

We remember an early "partner" we managed at a small company. The client frequently tossed around the term: "We are absolute partners in this venture!" The client was also one of the biggest companies in the world. The term "partner" was used freely during times of success. A great portion of our organization rallied around the term and would swap stories in the office about the latest meeting where they showered us with praise. However, during trying times the client always reverted back to the term "vendor," and the more inexperienced team members were always baffled by this behavior. We were never in a position of equal power, and early success blinded most of the team to the true nature of the relationship.

We believe client management advice to "create partnerships" is misguided – better to create relationships and good things will follow.

When you treat a client like a customer, they will treat you like a partner.

You Have Three Jobs

Job #1: Create relationships

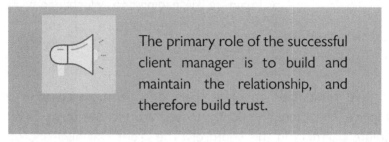

The primary role of the successful client manager is to build and maintain the relationship, and therefore build trust.

This sounds simple but belies a world of complexity. All the other roles and responsibilities of client management derive from this first principle. Without a solid relationship, you will never accomplish anything of value with your client.

We remain astounded that most client managers continue to view their relationships transactionally: What are we going to get from the client on this phone call, this email? Or they do not set up a regular cadence to touch base with their client, thinking, "Well, I haven't heard anything, so everything must be great!" Or worse yet, they look down on their client: "Can you believe how stupid these guys are?"

Without these foundational steps, you will never get to the level of building trust – and **trust is the foundation of all successful business transactions.**

This isn't to suggest other concerns aren't important, but without a strong foundation, your success will be limited to low-trust transactions. In Chapter 2, we'll review simple techniques you can implement today to deepen your relationships.

Job #2: Grow the client

We know too many client managers who react well to their client's demands, but don't consider their company's interest to grow the client. This kind of growth can take several directions – the introduction of new products or services, bringing your product to other divisions of the client, or organic growth of your existing client.

If you're an executive, you're saying to yourself, "Hey, shouldn't that be the first priority of client management?" We would agree, but without the strong foundation of a relationship, your ability to advance your agenda with a client will not matter. We've seen many CFOs who cannot understand why a client is not growing and yet do not understand the context of the relationship.

In Chapter 4, we'll review setting a foundation that will enable you to grow.

Job #3: Service the client (everything that is not Job #1 and Job #2)

Managing the tasks and demands that get between you and your first two objectives is a job in itself. We'll cover all of these as well.

Client management vs. sales

Unlike a traditional sales representative, remember that you have three roles:

1. Create relationships.
2. Grow the client.
3. Service the client.

Because of these sometimes conflicting roles, every client manager is faced with a dilemma: Unless you make growth your highest priority (other than the relationship itself), inevitably the service tasks and requests will take over your daily life... and eventually replace your first and second priorities.

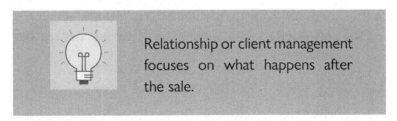

Relationship or client management focuses on what happens after the sale.

This may be more applicable to certain industries than others. For example, products such as commodities or consulting services are sold as one-offs that may not have an existing daily relationship component and may be more sales oriented. On the other hand, products like software, outsourced services, or insurance all require an ongoing relationship with a client that has a daily, weekly, and quarterly cadence of interactions. In addition, we generally mean business-to-business (B2B) interactions, although many of these techniques could apply to consumer or non-profit interactions as well. This book will help new client managers understand the role and learn how to make it a meaningful, impactful part of any organization.

The Principles of Client Management

Where does that leave us? What is the roadmap that will guide us on the journey of client management? How do we deal with each new type of situation?

After many years managing multiple account teams, we believe that success in business is based on trust. Trust is built through a strong foundation in personal character. People who exhibit character will naturally be successful at whatever they achieve. So how do we put this into action?

We can't prepare you for every encounter, but following these principles will demonstrate your commitment to character. When you are faced with a business client management challenge, remember the six Principles of Client Management:

1. Seek to understand, then to be understood.
2. We need each other. Our relationship is not a zero-sum game.
3. Concentrate on material issues, not the small stuff...
4. ...but on the other hand, if it's easy, then just do it.
5. Email is a low-context form of communication. For important things, use something better.
6. Always start by assuming the other side has the best intentions.

Seek to understand, then to be understood

We borrow this directly from Steven Covey's self-improvement masterpiece, *The Seven Habits of Highly Effective People*. We are all driven by our own agenda, and client-facing businesspeople tend to be more driven than most. Often, we can't get out of our own way and actively listen to other people. If you believe Job #1 is building relationships, then the most important thing you can do is actively listen to others. We'll translate this into tactics in Chapters 2 and 11.

Our relationship is not a zero-sum game

You and your client need each other. We cannot count the number of senior executives we've heard talk a big game about the need to get tough with the client. Attempting to project strength and toughness, they view the client as the enemy. "Hell no, we're not going to agree to that in the contract!" or "We need to tell these guys to go screw themselves!"

Many executives (and even some client managers) believe their business acumen is burnished when they demonstrate that they don't need the client's business. Of course, this begs the question why they are a client in the first place! To be clear, there will be times when it is in the company's best interest to say no, but when and how to say no should be considered carefully. We'll talk about how to think about negotiations and manage the "No" in Chapter 3.

Concentrate on material issues, not the small stuff... but on the other hand, if it's easy, then just do it

One of the worst insults a client manager can receive is when a business executive (or anyone not on the front lines with the client) refers to them as an "order taker" – meaning someone who reacts to client requests but does not drive strategic or growth conversations with clients.

Those small client requests for additional features, reporting, certifications, extra work, etc., can quickly overwhelm your more important objectives of client management and growth. On the other hand, managing client requests in a structured way is the only way to ensure the relationship is on solid footing. The little things that keep clients happy are the oil in the engine of the relationship. Those requests should not only be actioned, but they should be completed with vigor and a positive attitude. When these requests come up they will often require work by other parts of the organization. As the client manager, it is important for you to articulate internally why this is important and how it will help accomplish your strategic imperatives. In Chapter 3, we'll discuss simple ways to handle disagreement and communicate positive action.

Email is a low-context form of communication

For important things, use something better. This is an often-repeated conversation with beginning client managers:

> **Boss:** "Hey, has Client XYZ gotten back to us about whether we can do task ABC on project X?"
>
> **Client manager:** "Not yet, I sent them an email. Not sure if they understood it."
>
> **Boss:** "Well, do you think you could call them?"
>
> **Client manager:** "Well, I wasn't sure if it was that urgent."
>
> **Boss:** "Well, we're talking about it, so it must be urgent, right?"
>
> **Client manager:** (Awkward silence)

Email (and other forms of written, asynchronous communication like Slack, Chatter, MS Teams, SMS, etc.) are tremendous advances in business productivity. And all of them lack the context, nuance, and urgency of voice or face-to-face communications. Humans communicate much more information non-verbally – tone, body language – than they do in any other way. We'll dive deep into communications in Chapter 11.

Always start by assuming the other side has the best intentions

Many business misunderstandings and relationship failures are easily avoidable if either party takes the time to consider the other side's intent. When a client asks for better pricing, more services, or faster delivery, it's very unlikely they ask out of malice, and even less likely that they want to harm your organization. They perceive a business need that they think you can solve. When you start with assuming good intentions, you are more likely to be open to hearing the root cause of the request – and more likely to arrive at a creative solution together.

However, you shouldn't be willfully blind to the reality that clients may not always have your best interests at heart. In fact, we've seen many times when a client makes their vendor especially useful by scapegoating them to their own senior executives. This is human nature – we'll discuss some tricks to manage such situations throughout the book.

We want to emphasize that you should **start** by assuming that intentions are good – knowing that in the end, they may not be. With this technique, you open yourself up to better listening and creative client solutions. We'll discuss this relationship basic in Chapter 2 and how it relates to your personal leadership in Chapter 7.

Principles of Client Management

 Seek to understand, then to be understood.

 We need each other. Our relationship is not a zero-sum game.

 Concentrate on material issues, not the small stuff...

 ...but on the other hand, if it's easy, then just do it.

 Email is a low-context form of communication. For important things, use something better.

 Always start by assuming the other side has the best intentions.

Job #1:
Build and
Maintain
the Client
Relationship

Chapter 1:
We Have Relationships with People, Not Entities

We once worked at a technology company that had an extremely large, global organization as a client. The relationship was challenging, to say the least. Our performance with the client was uneven and created tension within the relationship. The client's attitude toward our young company drove all our emotional ups and downs. When the relationship was sound, we felt unconquerable, but when the relationship was tough, we were despondent. Suffice it to say that at any given time there was always a reason to believe we were moments away from being "in the doghouse" with this particular client.

Fast forward several years and a different picture emerges. Each of the individual client relationships we formed during those years continue to this day. In fact, these individuals are some of our closest professional friends. Most have moved on to other endeavors, but the relationship endures. Even when our company failed to deliver for them, what these individuals remember about us is our behavior, how we conducted ourselves, and how we always strove for excellence even if we did not always deliver. They knew that our intentions were pure and honest. In fact, these clients have even helped us grow our own careers – recommending us for client management roles at their new companies!

Why would that be when it was such a troubled relationship? It's because we always followed the golden rule:

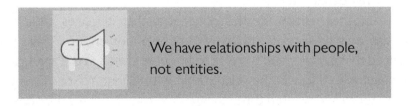

We have relationships with people, not entities.

Our relationship never was with the "big client" – the relationships were with the individuals who worked there. We also worked from a position of transparency, which built trust.

As client management leaders, we'll ask our team, "How's it going with client organization X?" It is in fact a bit of a trick question – you cannot have a relationship with an organization, only individual people. A strong client manager's answer will speak to the most strategic individual relationships they currently support.

Your Relationship with Your Client is Like a Bank Account

Our protégés often ask, "How do I actually build a relationship – what do I do?" The answer is deceptively simple:

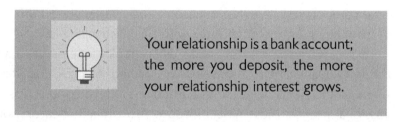

Your relationship is a bank account; the more you deposit, the more your relationship interest grows.

It may seem like an oddly reductionist view of relationships – equating them to a bank account? This is not a new idea, but what we are suggesting is to apply it in a B2B context.

We believe this is the right model for a simple reason: A bank account is a tangible entity, not soft and squishy like a relationship. We also find that if you ask client managers about the status of their relationship with another entity, they will say, "Fine." If you ask how full the relationship bank account is, you get a much different (and more realistic) answer. This approach puts the relationship in far more well-defined terms.

Another reason for this concept is that it makes clear that we can only have relationships with people, not entities. Have you noticed that people tend to refer to business clients in the aggregate? For example, "How is the relationship with Client Y?" or "Client X called today and wanted three things." You cannot have a relationship with a legal entity. Legal entities do not have hands and cannot pick up the phone to call. Deposits and withdrawals can only be made with individuals, not entities or groups of people. And hence all relationships must be built on a personal level, not at the entity level.

Make Account Deposits

In a business context, what counts as a deposit? The good news is it can be almost anything from a personal to a professional deliverable. A task completed, new initiative delivered, or milestone achieved can all add to the relationship. Without knowing your industry, it is difficult to make a concrete suggestion, but a good rule of thumb is that **a deposit is equal to perception minus expectation.**

In other words, delivering your contractually agreed-upon product or service on time, safely, and with few errors is probably not a deposit. Doing it consistently for months or years (above industry standard) probably is a deposit. Sending get-well flowers for a client's spouse who is in the hospital is absolutely a deposit because it is unexpected. Some new client managers are surprised to learn that "doing your job" does not lead to relationship deposits by itself.

In fact, we would suggest that the most important relationship deposits are unsolicited and for no business reason. A simple note or phone call to check in to "make sure you're getting what you need" can be incredibly powerful. If you are ever at a loss for the next step with a client, ten minutes brainstorming on the topic of "How can I make a deposit?" can bring your relationship to the next level. These can be very simple moments such as "Congratulations to your sports team for their victory," or "I saw the hurricane forecast. You have family in that area, don't you? Is everyone okay?" Thinking beyond the confines of the day-to-day relationship or operations goes a long way.

The next level of power is to marry this type of relationship development with solid operational delivery of your product or service. Client managers who can execute for clients **and** make relationship deposits maintain customers for life.

The 7:1 Ratio

There is one area where the bank account analogy breaks down: Unlike a bank account, if you stop making deposits, you slowly lose your relationship equity. The good news is that it leaves the account more slowly than you can build it back, but all relationships require some level of deposits.

Another slight difference: a real bank account takes deposits and withdrawals in objective criteria – money. Relationship bank accounts are subjective and susceptible to the self-serving bias – the tendency we all have to overestimate our accomplishments and abilities and underestimate our weaknesses or liabilities. This implies that you are likely to overestimate how many deposits you have contributed to a relationship. Also, clients do not make equivalencies when something goes wrong: "Yes, Mr. Client, I know you are upset, but I sent you a birthday card... so we're good?" Most, if not all, deposits and withdrawals will be unspoken – and best that way. There is no way to maintain an even score.

For all these reasons, make deposits to withdrawals in a 7:1 ratio. At first glance, this may seem absurd. You may ask, "What kind of relationship is it where I am giving more than the other person?"

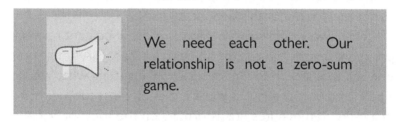

We need each other. Our relationship is not a zero-sum game.

If you think in terms of zero-sum (I win, you lose, and vice versa), then the 7:1 ratio will be nonsensical. Most of the deposits you will make in your relationship bank account are not zero-sum. Think of all of the ways you can add to a relationship today that are quick and cost almost nothing:

- Send your client a birthday card.
- Check in on the status of a joint initiative.
- Respond with gratitude for their customer survey feedback.

- Share the latest industry trends.
- Ask how a particular product feature is working.
- Inquire about their hobbies and recreational interests.

Adding to your relationship balance in any of these ways is a win-win. By investing at a 7:1 ratio, you take your relationship to a new level and ensure that when you need to make a withdrawal, you have the relationship equity to do so.

Manage Withdrawals

We could simply say that withdrawals are just the opposite – when expectations exceed results. A more realistic view is that as a client manager, you are probably already keenly aware of when your organization's delivery fails to meet expectations. It might be expressed as direct feedback, anger, or stony silence. Many of these withdrawals will be inadvertent… let's face it, who wants to do a bad job for their customer?

As a client manager, you have to understand that eventually a withdrawal will be required, and **it is your responsibility to deliver the bad news to the client.** No other member of your team can do this, whether they're in operations or product management. Worse yet, you must take responsibility for the withdrawal – in other words, you cannot soften the blow by saying, "Well, 'they' are making me increase prices on you," or "If I had my way, we would do this better, but…" You own the outputs of your organization because you are a representative of that organization. We'll discuss some techniques for communicating withdrawals in later chapters.

When you deliver relationship deposits far in excess of withdrawals, you can make those withdrawals with intent – because it is the right thing to do for your business overall – and feel good about doing it because you have worked hard to make the relationship balance positive.

Required withdrawals

There are times as a business leader when your business interests require a withdrawal from a customer. You may need to increase pricing, discontinue a product line because it is obsolete, or inform the client that the feature they require won't be ready on time.

Regardless of the reason, one day your company will ask you to make a withdrawal. However, since you've been making deposits at a 7:1 ratio in advance, you are in a much better position to weather the storm.

Yes, your client will be upset and may express that in a variety of ways (yelling, stony silence, passive aggressiveness). When that happens, accept it for what it is and be glad. Why glad?

Because the central truth is that the opposite of love is not hate, it is indifference. As long as your customer is upset, they are at least engaged in the problem.

If you deliver terrible news to the client and they are indifferent... well, it's time to worry, because they just signed with your competitor!

A note about winning

We're sure this isn't you, but it's worth noting for some client managers. We've seen occasions when client managers get in the mode of winning an argument with the client, particularly during special-event processes such as contract renewal or execution of a complex project. Usually this manifests itself as returning to the office and telling everyone, "Yeah, we really told those guys how it is!" or "They dropped their pants like a rodeo clown!" – some type of boasting. Of course, they have temporarily forgotten that **we need each other; our relationship is not a zero-sum game.** Winning generally means the client is likely completely re-evaluating the relationship, and you are operating with a negative relationship bank account.

Even worse is the scenario where you and the client are discussing compliance with the existing contract. Reviewing the finer points of pricing accuracy or Service Level Agreement compliance is fine on occasion, but if the conversation begins to frequently reference the contract, you are in deeply negative territory. We've seen client relationships so incredibly awful that neither party will do much for the other unless explicitly spelled out in a contract. Needless to say, this is the end of that relationship. We had a mentor who used to say, "The best thing that can possibly happen is the day you sign a contract, and you stick it in a drawer, never to be seen again until renewal." We could not agree more. If you mention the contract to your client, you are by definition making a withdrawal — so use with extreme caution.

We worked with an individual who negotiated a massive contract with a large client when he was with a previous company. He did an incredible job of "winning," so much so that when he joined our company, the same client (which the two companies had in common) would not talk to him or allow him on-site for close to six months! In his previous negotiation, he knew he had a competitive advantage and leveraged it to the greatest extent possible — a great example of a short-term win but long-term loss.

Remember: People build relationships with people, not entities. If entities developed relationships, then this transition would have been perfectly smooth, but unfortunately that was not the case here. If you feel like you are winning with a client, be careful — you may, in fact, be making relationship withdrawals.

Tactics

1 Never tell your boss "the client called" or "the client wants X" without also delineating who at the client is making the request. "Client Co." is a big building filled with people. The building did not pick up the phone and dial to make a request.

2 Do not refer to groups within the client: "The client's customer care team wants us to develop a new feature." More accurately: "Steve in the customer care team wants us to develop a new feature." Making a decision about a business investment disassociated from the individual making the request means you will lack crucial context to make the decision. Do not abstract.

3 When evaluating who at the client made the request, it is critical to distinguish between who picked up the phone to make the request and who originated the request.

4 Any major events with your client (e.g., an acquisition, restructuring, new leadership) will have consequences for individuals at the client and potentially the entity's relationships overall. Client managers must seek to understand all impacts at a micro and macro level – be prepared to speak to these potential impacts at a moment's notice.

5 Know the background and context for individuals at your client – their interests, background, and attitude toward your company.

Chapter 2:
Create Connections and
Seek to Understand

We were very excited about the upcoming event we were planning for our clients: attending a world-class sporting event sold out years in advance. With the hard part of procuring the tickets completed, we aligned the schedules of numerous incredibly busy, high-ranking executives. To make it happen, we worked with the executives' administrative assistants. Needless to say, they are just as busy as their executives, and since this wasn't necessarily work-related, it felt like busy work. Eventually, the stress reared its head in the form of frustration and terse phone calls. We were frustrated as well – trying to build client relationships and yet on the receiving end of administrative assistants' tirades. The executives frequently upbraided us about business matters – but did we have to take this from the admins as well? We were confronted with making one of three choices:

1. Call the executives and ask them to get their administrative assistants in order (most new client managers' response).
2. Respond in kind (e.g., escalate with the admin by responding with the same tone and frustration).
3. Treat the administrative assistants like clients and focus on the solution.

We chose the third option, and we even went so far as to get the administrative assistants souvenirs from the event.

Everyone showed up on time, and the event went off without a hitch. The executives had a phenomenal time. Far more importantly, by treating the admins as clients equal to their bosses, we ended up with long-term preferential treatment. Our calls always got answered and our messages were at the top of the stack. In addition, those executives would alert us when one of our competitors would come to visit, usually with a dismissive story about their lack of capability.

The pain of setting up the relationship-building event slowly faded as we realized what we had gained was absolutely priceless.

Every Interaction Matters

We used to have a boss who said, "Every client interaction is a sales interaction." He didn't mean every time you talked to someone you needed to sell something. Instead, each interaction with a client company, no matter the person or role you are interacting with, is important to your success. It may seem obvious; we all know the Golden Rule. But we're constantly surprised by how people forget this important maxim when actually visiting a client. Treating the administrator in the front office any differently than the CEO will reflect poorly – assume that every person you work with will talk to every other person in the organization. When you spot an opportunity to add value and make their lives easier, take the time to do so – it will pay dividends later.

We know executives at several organizations who are much more interested in how you interact with their staff than how you interact with them. One even mentioned, "Whenever I do business with someone, I always take them to dinner so I can see how they treat the server." We know of a CEO who always takes potential new hires to breakfast, arrives early, and instructs the wait staff to botch the order. When asked why he simply said, "I want to see how the candidate responds."

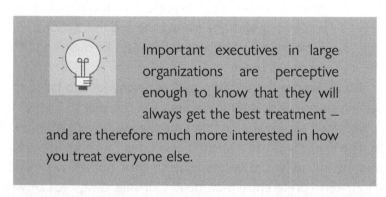

Important executives in large organizations are perceptive enough to know that they will always get the best treatment – and are therefore much more interested in how you treat everyone else.

Turn your world view upside down: Treat the people you believe to be the least important in the organization as the most important, and you will be the client manager to remember. Furthermore, that person may one day occupy their boss' seat.

The executives who make decisions will hear about it – guaranteed. Here are some great places to start:

- The client's customer support or servicing staff – anyone from your client who interacts directly with customers, including call center staff, floor salespeople, and operations teams.
- The client's back-office teams – accounting, finance, HR, etc. Treat them as valued partners and you will be differentiated from regular vendors.
- And most importantly, the client's executive assistant. In the modern era, these folks act less like gatekeepers and more like general counselors/chiefs of staff to your executive clients. Their opinion matters, and they are the most likely to get feedback from everyone else in the organization.

We can't emphasize it enough: When building client relationships, start with the understanding that every interaction matters. Everyone on your relationship map is a person worth your attention and investment.

Learn Your Client

Think a little bit about the clients you manage today. Do you know their personal background? Do you know about their hobbies or interests? Unless you are already an exceptional client manager, it's unlikely you do.

In business environments driven by technology and social media, the great irony is that now we create even less connection to others. The black rectangle in your pocket enjoys all the attention people used to give to other human beings. This has a profoundly negative impact on relationships.

But within that, you have a massive opportunity to turbocharge your career and differentiate yourself.

> Seek to understand, then to be understood. Job #1 is to build the relationship. No coincidence that both are first and foremost.

By putting these things first (even before your own agenda) you will materially change the nature of your client relationship and build trust. Many businesspeople, particularly those who fancy themselves focused only on the "hard" business skills (finance, analysis, strategy), ignore these fundamental tenets at their peril.

Think of these "soft skills" as something you can create as a checklist — making it a "to do" with each client. This technique translates a soft skill into an objective with a concrete result, not unlike many consumer products companies — they collect data on you and your preferences because they want to build a relationship. Therefore, if you are in the business of managing relationships, learn basic facts about your clients.

Let's start with the minimum:

Topic	What you need to know	Why
Professional background	The overall trajectory of their career. Bonus points if you know their last three employers. The good news is that LinkedIn makes this relatively easy. (You have linked with them on LinkedIn already, haven't you?)	To understand their frame of reference, you need to know where they've been and how that might affect their thinking about your business.

Topic	What you need to know	Why
Hobbies and interests	Know 1-2 interests outside of the work environment. No need to be invasive, but know enough to be able to ask follow-up questions.	Building the relationship. Most people are absolutely dying for you to interact with them on a human level at work. Use this information to understand them better as people.
Their birthday	(Self-explanatory)	Again, to use to build the relationship. Also a great opportunity to reach out to clients and touch base outside of a business need.
Assistant's information	Name and number. Bonus points for knowing something about them.	Remember the story at the beginning of this chapter?
Their point of view on your product/ service/ relationship	Whether they are a supporter, neutral, or detractor.	For the obvious reasons.

Topic	What you need to know	Why
Social network presence	If they have a public social media presence (e.g., social media clearly meant to drive their business or LinkedIn profiles) then a link to that account is fine. Personal accounts (family photos, college parties, photos of their scrimshaw collection) require more thought – more on that later.	Used with caution, this is a valuable source of intelligence about the strategic direction of their business.
Physical address of the business	Both the headquarters and any satellite offices where your actual clients work.	Holiday gift baskets or cards (important!), formal invitations, etc.
Their kids' names	And their approximate age. Knowing something about their interests is an added plus.	This one might surprise you – but we would argue this is the most important on the list. We have yet to find even the most hardened executive who does not respond warmly when asked about their children.

We would highly recommend if your organization has a Customer Relationship Management (CRM) system that you create a log of these important details. Most out-of-the-box systems will capture some of these details (like addresses and social media links) but not the other information that is important to building a relationship. Ask your CRM administrator to add these fields. We love technology when it enables our primary mission of building relationships!

We're not suggesting you collect personal details like background and kids' names so you can pretend to be interested and fool them into building a relationship. Instead, collect personal information and actually be interested in the responses. One senior executive told us a great story: In a senior leadership meeting, the CEO (widely known as a terrible people leader) asked, "How can we get our employees to think we care about them?" The executive replied, "Maybe we should start by actually caring about them." Absurdly funny and absolutely true.

Personal facts are merely foundational elements – alone, they do not form a relationship. As a foundation, they will help support the rest of the relationship we are about to build.

The First Five Minutes

The web-based screen share is running, the conference call is working, and we just listed out the agenda. It's scheduled for an hour. The client just wasted ten minutes talking about their weekend. We have seven agenda items to cover regarding the new product rollout. Your boss is really anxious you cover number five on the list because it's one of his objectives for the year. You're thinking to yourself, "I really need to get this moving along so we can cover all of the items!" You know the client has some concerns left over from the last call, but we just don't have the time to deal with that right now!

Sound familiar? We're all pressed for time, particularly when we manage multiple clients. In business, we're often laser-focused on our objectives, our metrics.

When we do meetings right, we're very prepared and have the right messages, great story, and killer slides. And that's important! Unfortunately, all of that great preparation and focus on results can often get in the way of a fundamental objective:

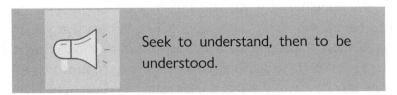

Seek to understand, then to be understood.

The good news here is that releasing your agenda gives you a reason for another near-term touch point.

In Steven Covey's highly readable 1989 bestseller *The Seven Habits of Highly Effective People,* he created a timeless framework for self-improvement.[1] While he rightly spends most of the book discussing character development, he also focuses on managing others. We borrow his classic concept of seeking to first understand others before turning your attention to your own interests. The primary goal of this type of listening is true empathy. In other words, don't listen with the judgments that we usually apply to what others say, but rather make a true effort to understand another's emotions. We'll borrow this concept throughout.

We recommend a very practical application of this concept for every client manager. **Seek to understand – in the first five minutes.** In other words, at the beginning of every interaction with a client, begin with them, not you. If speaking to a client casually, this can be as simple as asking about a topic they care about. One of our favorites is the very simple, "How is business?" Or better yet, ask a specific question about their interests, how their children are (by name, of course), or the results of their basketball game.

Think about how much more powerful that is than the usual conversation starters ("How are you?" "Fine."). By actually starting with attempting to understand, we build strong, powerful relationships. In Chapter 9, we'll discuss meeting preparation, but never forget the strongest start to any meeting is putting understanding the client first.

Often, this can sound like, "I know our agenda today covers various topics, but let's start with this: Anything on your mind we need to make sure we cover today?" Seems obvious, except that it

---

[1] The next time you find yourself clicking on an article titled "The Seven Things You MUST DO to Advance Your Career" or some other clickbait listicle – STOP – and buy this book instead.

almost never happens. Differentiate yourself by making this simple tip your best practice. Begin with understanding others and putting their needs first.

Business Etiquette is About More Than Forks

There's probably no phrase more fussy-sounding than "business etiquette" (it brings to mind a thirteen-year-old's cotillion) – but that aside, what does it really mean? Rather than thinking in terms of using the correct fork,[2] think more about using micro-interactions to build relationships, and therefore build trust.

There are three broad categories of business etiquette that the professional client manager needs to actively manage: putting people at ease, no woobies (more on this later), and interacting with senior executives.

Put people at ease

If you are new in your client management career, you're probably unaware that many of your counterparts at your client's company are not as self-assured as they may appear. In addition, many of the folks on the other side of the table are craving human kindness and interaction – particularly if they work at a larger organization. The larger the company is, the less likely there is any type of human touch from their peers or their boss.

We often see a new client manager kick off a meeting with a long, awkward silence before the meeting officially begins. Or run out of things to discuss at a client dinner once business is concluded. Or – the most dreadful of all – canoodling with their smartphone in the presence of a client.

If you are the client manager, it is your responsibility to put everyone at ease. This is often surprising to those who come to client management from a non-sales part of an organization. It requires you to mentally pull back from what you are about to deliver (which you are already nervous about) and focus on someone else. We expect salespeople to be "sales-y" in all situations and usually defer to them

---

[2] For the record, we don't know which fork is correct.

for that role. However, if you own the account post-sale (and no salesperson is present), it becomes the responsibility of the client manager. This is not a nice-to-have or soft skill – this is an absolute requirement for building relationships and trust.

Always have three to four prebaked client interaction points you can use in any situation. We've provided a list of value-neutral questions in the Tactics section of this chapter to get you started. To further your ability to put people at ease with prebaked discussion topics, regularly read at least three publications: a general-interest news daily/weekly (*New York Times*, *Time*, etc.), a business-oriented publication (*Wall Street Journal*, *Bloomberg*, *Economist*), and at least one industry trade journal.

Topics to avoid

One caveat: Stay away from the clearly inappropriate topics, like politics or religion. This seems obvious, but we have seen situations where clients will actually bring up these topics. As you already know, most business workplaces generally discourage political discussions, and most advice on the issue is to avoid the topic of conversation altogether. But what if your client wants to have that conversation? This makes it a much more delicate matter.

Fred once had a client who, out of the blue, brought up a recent presidential campaign and asked his opinion. Fred was not sure if this was a test or an innocent attempt to make conversation, but he did know that this subject was off limits. Fred simply replied, "While I have seen most of the current headlines, I haven't had a chance to really dig in to understand the nuances. Until I get a chance to do that, I will have to pass. I don't want to speak to things where I am ill-informed." The client then went on to share his opinions, many of which Fred did not agree with. Fred's agreement or lack thereof was of no consequence in this situation.

But what if you really do want to discuss politics with your client? Our recommendation: don't. Even if you suspect you are both politically aligned, you might be wrong and in for an unpleasant surprise. In that instance, you may feel differently about your client after the conversation, negatively impacting the relationship and reducing trust. Since trust is your primary goal as a client manager, there is no upside to this conversation, even if you suspect alignment may deepen the relationship. Remember, political views are like musical taste – you can't convince someone else to like what you like through persuasion. Also, otherwise perfectly wonderful people can have different tastes than you in music (and in politics). We know you have all of John Tesh's recorded catalog, but it is not likely you will convince us of its merits.

While they may ask for your opinion, what they are really seeking is confirmation of theirs. There are several tactful ways to get out of these situations:

1. Acknowledge the question, evade answering, and gracefully change the subject. For example, a client asks your opinion about the president's stance on a current issue. Your reply: "That is interesting. Funny enough my brother was asking me about that last night, but I haven't had the chance to read up on it. I would hate to answer without having all the details. Do you have any siblings?"

2. Answer with a non-answer: "I can see both sides of the conversation and am very interested to see where they land on this policy."

3. Politely let them know that this is off-limits: "I have a friend who used to love debating about politics, but it always ended in an argument. I thought to myself, 'This isn't a lot of fun.' So I tend to shy away. Now if you want to talk about the greatest running back of all time, bring it on."

We recommend only engaging with listening, even if you agree with your client. You can limit your engagement to understanding your client's passion but maintaining neutrality ("I can tell you feel strongly about this," "Hopefully they can work it out," "It's definitely an important issue."). It's likely your client will understand your reticence to engage and move on from the topic. If they do not move on, view it as a challenge to your non-judgmental listening skills. The act of listening without replying can be very therapeutic for the amateur politician and might earn you a considerable relationship deposit in the bargain.

No woobies

It should seem obvious, but it's inescapable. We often see junior client managers intently tapping away or scrolling on their laptop or phone in the presence of a client. We know a senior executive who has recently begun to ask at the beginning of every meeting for "no woobies" – meaning, no security blankets (à la 1983's *Mr. Mom*) in the form of screens. She perceives (correctly, we believe) that her team is using technology as a filter to avoid the hard work of one-on-one human interaction.

We recommend a simple technique to manage your personal technology while at a client site: **Think of your technology as being mildly radioactive.** Put your phone and tablet in your briefcase, even your fitness watch. Remove the temptation from your grasp. You may need to use it for a specific purpose (your laptop, for example, for a presentation), but the more you are exposed, the more harm caused.

In our experience, the quickest way to be labeled a millennial (or some other innocent-sounding yet secretly pejorative age-related label) is to access technology at inappropriate times during a meeting. For the record, every age cohort and every type of person is now guilty of this behavior – but we do observe that more seasoned leaders tend to realize that the major work of their day-to-day is building relationships. Imitate that behavior to put others at ease. Disengage from screens and engage directly.

A note about notetaking

Today's academic pipeline encourages the use of computers, especially for notetaking. It's often a surprise to early-career people that this behavior is simply unacceptable in the business world. Therefore, our recommendation is simple: If you are a meeting participant, do not take notes on your computer. Ever. We know that "It's more efficient!" and "It makes it easier to track the notes later!" Regardless, taking electronic notes in a meeting (and the associated keyboard clacking) will reduce trust and make people uneasy – the exact opposite of what you are trying to achieve. There are many reasons why this is true, but two stand out:

1. If you are typing during a meeting, the other participants do not know whether you are participating, messaging with a friend, or watching cat videos.[3]

2. It will be almost impossible to interact successfully with the other participants because you are so busy typing.

The net effect is that you appear disengaged, regardless of whether that was your intention.

Strategies for note taking

- If you must have digital copies of your notes, use a Rocketbook or similar technology.
- You can write things down in a notebook with a pen and later upload a scan of the document to your computer via email, Dropbox, or numerous other integrated services. They even have OCR technology now – optical character recognition – which can transcribe the notes for you.

You might be granted an exception to this rule if you are in a large meeting and the designated note-taker. But in this case, you are no longer a meeting participant. As a client manager, you are likely either leading the meeting or at least participating... so no woobies!

A word about video conferencing

The advice in this chapter still holds true even if you are using technology to facilitate the interaction (i.e., video conferencing or web conferencing). We love these kinds of technologies because they are high-context communications that allow face-to-face meetings without traveling. However, all the same caveats apply, perhaps even more. It may seem ironic to suggest not using technology during a meeting facilitated by video technology – but **anything that creates the perception of a distraction should not be a**

---

[3] We like cat videos also, just not during meetings.

part of the meeting. Be particularly careful with business-oriented messaging platforms such as Slack, Microsoft Teams, etc. Using these programs will be noticed, even if your video is off. Remember why the video conference was initiated in the first place: to facilitate human interaction, not to detract from it.

Interacting with Senior Executives

This is often a source of anxiety for those new to client management, especially early in their career. You can easily tell who the senior executive is in any meeting – just look at who everyone is staring at for affirmation throughout the meeting. Follow the eyes and you will see the prize.

When working with executives, remember that they are people and wish to be treated as such. Even the most accomplished senior executives are, at their core, human beings with the same wants and needs as everyone else. In fact, because they have achieved material success, they are even hungrier for normal human interaction – a real connection with others based on a genuine relationship and not based on need. Senior executives with real leadership talent already know that they are wealthy, important, or senior and don't need to be reminded. They are generally much more interested in achieving their business objectives.

Of course, this isn't to say this is true of all executives – many are vain, egotistical, and insecure. But we would argue that these recommendations are even more important in that scenario. With that said, always read the executive for a sense of humor and other cues from what they say or their body language. Are they pressed for time? Do they keep looking at the clock?

If you are just beginning your client management career, we have one primary recommendation: **To build confidence and trust when working with executives, avoid awkward, status-reinforcing micro-interactions.**

Why focus on the micro? Because as a practical matter, your interactions with very senior executives may be limited in scope and very brief. In addition, as a vendor, it is likely an executive will delegate primary responsibility for the relationship to a subordinate.

Therefore, it's critical to quickly establish trust (or in this case, avoid the opposite). To that end, we recommend the following tactics:

Don't focus all your energy on one person

Avoid focusing all your conversational energy on the executive(s) during meetings or other conversations. This is the most common mistake new client managers make. By focusing your energy on one person, you create two issues: One, the executive will likely begin to feel uncomfortable from too much eye contact/focused attention, and two, you will appear self-serving and alienate others in the room. We understand this is almost impossible if you are new in your career and feeling less secure.

One suggestion would be to picture your head is on a swivel (or bearings) and is "loose." Not only will you loosen up and become more comfortable, but you will also be more likely to direct your energy across all participants evenly. Like any good public speaker, you have to work the entire room, not one person or one side. Another suggestion: Consciously decide to put most of your energy into the "least important" person in the room. The inevitable magnetic draw of the "most important" person will lead to a greater sense of balance in the discussion.

Avoid statements that reinforce status or position

We see this quite often as well – in an effort to acknowledge the executive, people make statements like "Well, someone in your position shouldn't have to worry about..." or "A person like you should be well aware that..." Senior executives are already aware of their status.

A few years ago, the company John worked for brought in a new senior executive as part of an acquisition. The executive was actually CEO of his former company and well known within the industry. By happenstance, he sat next to John in the break room on a day with a catered lunch. John didn't know him at all and had no idea whether he had any context to current operations. Given the day-to-day chaos surrounding the merger, John decided to let the new senior executive initiate if he wanted to start a relationship. So

John sat silently and ate his lunch. The new executive did the same and left. He told John years later that the reason he respected John was because he wasn't needy for attention. Lesson learned: Better to not interact at all than to do so in a way that is insincere or totally conditioned by the other person's seniority.

Avoid elaborate courtesies (that you wouldn't do for anyone else)

Again, for the same reason as mentioned before – because it creates odd energy that minimizes trust. Early in Fred's career, he and a friend of his were approaching the headquarters of their company. The front door was heavy glass, and coincidentally they could see the CEO was about to exit. In a fit of overdone courtesy, Fred's friend pulled hard on the door to allow the CEO to exit, as though the CEO were a maharaja. The door only swung inward though, which caused Fred's friend to crash his body awkwardly into the glass (and earn an odd look from the CEO). While amusing (hilarious, really), it could have been avoided if his friend had interacted with the normal level of courtesy you would extend to anyone else.

Social Media and Client Management

Navigating the new world of social media as a client manager can be tricky. Do I friend my clients? If so, who? Will they feel rejected if I do not accept a friend/follow request? We do recommend discovering and monitoring the professional social media presences of your clients. For example, if your client has a work Instagram account, then checking on that account occasionally will be valuable. However, caution is warranted. Our guidance for social media is simple: Connecting in professional networks (such as LinkedIn) is fine; avoid connecting to clients on a personal level.

For example, if you control a social media account related to your business (your company's Facebook page, for example) then, by all means, connect to your clients. However, for your personal social media presence, we recommend avoiding client contact. The reason should be relatively obvious – your professional life and your personal life can be vastly different. More importantly, connecting to professional contacts can have unintended consequences. When your college roommate posts your best-ever keg stand (and tags you), now it is part of your client's daily updates. In addition, if you want to communicate something of a personal nature to your friends, connections to professional associates can be constraining. Best to avoid those issues.

What if you are already connected to a friend who becomes a client? This may be a judgment call – we recommend breaking the social media link. This may seem drastic. Consider how far apart your professional and private lives are when making this decision.

It is tempting to believe that connecting in personal networks will improve your business relationship, but that is generally not true. People in B2B relationships do not value their relationship with you more or less based on whether you are connected on social media. Since the risks outweigh the benefits, consider avoiding this.

Value-Neutral Conversation Starters

"Tell me about yourself."

It's a classic conversation starter for a good reason: It always works. You can branch off into anything mentioned. Diving deeper is as easy as using the simple, often overlooked: "Tell me more about that." Bonus: You can fill in some relationship details.

"How is business?"

Perhaps a bit more relevant for a senior leader or owner, but a sure-fire winner for that crowd. There is nothing they enjoy discussing more. As an added bonus, you might gather some insights that will help steer your next upsell opportunity.

"What major projects are you working on besides this one?"

Always applicable in technology or manufacturing, which has project-based work.

"How long have you worked at company X?"

If you have less time and don't want someone's life story, you might just ask about their current role and its scope.

"What do you think about (the latest industry trend)?"

This one requires a bit of knowledge about your client's industry. Of course, this isn't a problem for you because you subscribe to the trade journal for that industry and skim the headlines daily. You also subscribe to a regular business publication (*Wall Street Journal*, *Financial Times*, *The Economist*) for more general business updates, right? Both will enable you to craft questions relevant to your client. You don't need to be an expert to ask a question – and you might learn something.

"How's (your sports team) doing this year?"

We list this one last because, although a good conversation starter, it does not allow you to learn something new about your client. Unless you are in professional sports – and in that case, start with this one! Nonetheless, discussing something other than the business can strengthen the foundation you are building.

Chapter 3:
When It Gets Negative, Start by Assuming All Sides Have the Best Intentions

We often want quick solutions for relationship problems, but the reality is the solution often exists beyond the horizon. John once worked with a very large client where the relationship was so poor, there was no way to reconcile. The relationship was worth hundreds of millions of dollars, with massive risks to both sides to breach the contract. The two senior executive teams were not on the same page in terms of overall industry direction and strategy. The client very much wanted to manage the operations themselves and had built an entire internal strategy around doing so. About three months into John's tenure as the VP in charge of the relationship, the client informed him they were going to write his company out. John thought he'd made a serious career mistake! From that meeting, the level of trust on both sides plummeted to negative territory. In short, it was the worst client relationship situation he'd ever seen.

John's team made the decision to manage the relationship only on the tactical level – but to do an outstanding job nevertheless. They focused all of their efforts on the three areas they could control: on-time delivery, technology stability, and operational excellence. John's team knew they could never win at the strategic level, so they focused all their energy on the much smaller span of direct control.

Over the next three years, client satisfaction (as measured with a quarterly survey) moved from the 50's to the high 80's, as John's team delivered operational benefits. Meanwhile, the client continued to do their best to leave, and they even began to ask for John's help in the process. The executive teams stopped speaking; the two sides were as far apart as ever.

Unbeknownst to any of the team, there was a storm brewing – the 2008 financial crisis. It forced a reckoning across the industry about what was truly important, and it turns out that a crisis can focus the mind. After spending hundreds of millions of dollars to create a new system, the client realized the less risky course was to stay with their current vendor. And because John's team had worked so hard to make the service operationally excellent, the client had a solid reason to stay. And that is exactly what they did.

Total time for this journey: eight years. By taking ownership (even though much of the negative relationship equity was beyond his team's control) John was in an excellent position when the landscape shifted.

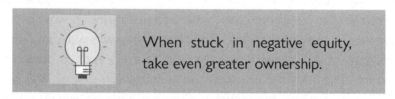

When stuck in negative equity, take even greater ownership.

Remember You're Jousting with the Dragon

We often see newer client managers framing issues in terms of equal partnership: "We've done so much for them! Just last week I went above and beyond, working 10 extra hours to ensure we fulfilled all of their orders. Now, they've asked for another huge favor this week... I'm going to tell them what they can do with it."

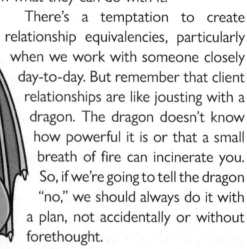

There's a temptation to create relationship equivalencies, particularly when we work with someone closely day-to-day. But remember that client relationships are like jousting with a dragon. The dragon doesn't know how powerful it is or that a small breath of fire can incinerate you. So, if we're going to tell the dragon "no," we should always do it with a plan, not accidentally or without forethought.

Let's review a few thought-starters for managing negative client interactions and situations where you have to disagree.

Concentrate on material issues, not small stuff

When managing negative client interactions, start by first considering whether you should disagree! In other words, is this disagreement something fundamentally important, or is it trivial? Sometimes it's not always easy to tell.

The question here is not whether you are right or wrong, but rather, "Does disagreeing advance the core interests of my organization?" Often, you will be encouraged by those around you (other functional areas perhaps) because your client is "asking for something ridiculous" or what they are asking for is "not in the contract." Or (our favorite), "It's the principle of the thing!" As your company's relationship representative to your client, you are not paid to manage principles – you are paid to manage interests!

As an example, a principle would be a value that we all cherish, like fairness or consistency. Fairness issues manifest as "what they are asking for is not fair to us." Consistency comes out as "they asked for X last week and now they want Y, which is totally different!" We would suggest that "fixing" these types of issues is a fool's errand and not a good use of time for the client manager.

We're taught from grade school that these should be the guiding values to live a decent life, and we are also taught to enforce those principles with others. It would be nice to be able to make our clients better people, but unfortunately, that is not within the purview of the client manager. Your role is to ensure you can leverage your relationship to accomplish the main three jobs with your client. If disagreeing with your client does not materially advance your primary company objectives, then it is highly likely you should think about not saying no.

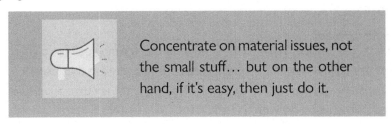

Concentrate on material issues, not the small stuff… but on the other hand, if it's easy, then just do it.

Often, the types of requests that violate standard principles are not material to the relationship and are really in the category of "easy" (meaning, not a lot of resources are required to execute). By saying yes to easy things, we make relationship deposits instead of withdrawals. With those in the bank, we can advance our much more material interests.

One of the most difficult parts of this thought process is that it is easy in a vacuum, but your coworkers do not exist in a vacuum. They will have thoughts and opinions about how to manage the client. In particular, execution teams often want to "push back"[1] on the client for all the aforementioned reasons.

Fred was once confronted with a decision about whether to attend a client meeting. It wasn't clear he needed to go, but he had his own reasons for doing so. Namely, he was new to the company and the relationship, and he wanted to attend the meeting to increase his technical acumen. However, his counterpart on the client's business side was not planning on attending the meeting. Furthermore, the counterpart had a very firm policy regarding the need to keep similar (equivalent) functions present at all meetings. Meaning, if Fred attended, then he would need to attend. The client was relatively hierarchical, with many unwritten rules around who goes to what meeting.

As Fred pushed to attend (which was a truly benign request) the emotion grew and created a great deal of strain. Adding to the complexity of the situation, Fred had internal teammates encouraging him to take control of the situation, let the client know that he was being irrational, and that Fred would attend. He let his ego take the bait. To Fred's peril, he did exactly what the client didn't want him to do, which created a completely unnecessary tense situation. It later required an about-face, groveling, and a few weeks of heavy-handed interaction on behalf of the client to ensure everyone knew who was in charge.

---

[1] In fact, the phrase "push back" should be the warning bell for a good client manager – it is an overused, stock business phrase that usually indicates the speaker wants to avoid a challenge, rather than a rational analysis of what to do with a client.

Multiple lessons learned:

1. Do not get caught up in winning. It never works.
2. Do not let internal associates appeal to your emotions and encourage behavior that is not absolutely aligned with your company's objectives. Your ego is irrelevant, the company's imperatives are always first and foremost. If this is a struggle for you, then client management may not be the right fit.

Take Greater Ownership

In the previous chapters, we covered tactics to move your client relationships into positive bank account territory. However, there are occasions where the relationship account is in negative territory and there is no pathway to bring it back to positive. We would argue that there is almost always a way to solve this dilemma, but it may require investment over a long period of time. Perhaps your client disagrees with your overall business strategy. Or your company's on-time delivery is so dismal the customer loses money, and your company is unwilling to invest to remediate. Or your client's senior executives have a poor personal relationship with your company's executives.

Our natural tendency in these situations is to give up because we "know we can never win with this client." We throw our hands up in frustration and tell everyone, "This company doesn't care about its customers." As frustrating as this can be, there is always hope. We like to remember Teddy Roosevelt's quote: "Do what you can, with what you have, where you are, right now." When you're in a negative relationship equity situation, you want to believe nothing can be done because it relieves you of responsibility (and ownership) of the challenge.

When faced with negative relationship equity, take greater ownership of the client

Why? Because situations change, and you want to be prepared to take advantage when that happens. In addition, as the client manager, this is the only way to unequivocally ensure you understand the root cause of the state of the relationship. Ownership, in this case, might not look like bringing the relationship balance to positive, but it is a start.

More importantly, it is likely that the leadership team at your company is aware of why the relationship is poor and what your company is doing (or not doing) to cause the issues. By taking greater ownership of the outcomes, you will endear yourself to your leadership team by attempting to do what you can with what you have. They understand that the situation may be "impossible," but if you work on your relationship fundamentals, you stand a better chance of being prepared when the situation shifts in your favor. However, the probability that your leadership's understanding is high is not guaranteed. Taking complete ownership also allows you to ensure thorough and accurate communication with your executive team, eliminating uncertainty on anyone's behalf.

There is another possibility here: Your leadership team absolutely blames you for the poor relationship! Whether your fault or not, sometimes the larger the organization, the less likely it is that senior leadership truly understands all of the relevant issues. If that's the case, you might as well push harder to achieve a 7:1 ratio because you own the problem whether you like it or not!

Get to the Root Cause

Often, clients in B2B relationships have to make a withdrawal from your relationship bank account (and probably will not think about it nearly as much as you will after reading this book). They might not agree to your contract terms, performance metrics, pricing, etc. – any business relationship offers many ways to object. It is tempting to believe the party on the other side of the table is the one telling you "no" and to believe the worst from that interaction. Either they are deliberately obstinate or just want you to fail as a client manager!

You probably don't know the real reason, so get to the root cause. The more forceful the "no," the more likely the other party is responding to an incentive in their organization that they do not control.

Is it Fundamental Attribution Error?

Most of us are prone to **Fundamental Attribution Error** – a concept from social psychology that describes our tendency to emphasize a person's internal character rather than external factors in explaining other people's behavior. In other words, if a client tells us something we don't want to hear, we are very likely to believe it is because of their personal characteristics (e.g., they are unpleasant, lazy, uncaring, etc.) rather than believe that the driver of their behavior is their context, the external forces acting on them.

Fundamental Attribution Error is often a more comforting story than reality. It allows us to blame someone else's personal characteristics for outcomes rather than the situation. We often forget that (almost) everyone takes orders from someone else. Western cultures are particularly prone to this fallacy because we all believe we are individuals who drive action in the world, rather than allowing the world to dictate action to us.

We once had a client who was by far the most unpleasant, unlikeable individual we had ever encountered. We were providing a technology service to his company, and he was the manager of the product. Since most of his product was outsourced to a vendor, he felt he had less control than he would have had otherwise, which led him to be hypercritical. He often lamented that he was "disappointed" with our work. In fact, it's fair to say "disappointed" was his favorite word – he used it liberally. It was a challenge to motivate the team to perform for him, as everyone knew we would not measure up in the end. We suffered until he eventually left our client in a corporate restructuring.

In an effort to help him after the restructuring, we hired him for a consulting project. In the course of that (and getting to know him better), we learned that outside of that particular work environment, he actually was a very good person. The relationship continued to grow. As he became more comfortable with us, he eventually revealed that during the time he worked for our customer, he was routinely abused by senior management. Every Friday his boss would call him in for a two-hour meeting and excoriate his work, shouting and screaming – absolutely terrible bullying behavior. When he recalled the experience, he seemed visibly shaken, and we could tell the meetings were threatening and a cause of high emotional distress. Suffice to say, all along we were suffering from Fundamental Attribution Error – believing his character was the issue, when in reality his environment was the driver for his actions. We should have done a much better job of **seeking to understand, getting to the root cause,** and **starting by assuming the other side has the best intentions.**

There is a second lesson here: All organizations (especially large ones) go through reorganizations frequently. If you wait long enough, your day-to-day contact will change and most likely your executive sponsorship will as well. Be prepared for the change by taking massive ownership of the client regardless of the level of their relationship bank account.

Don't Just Say No

In addition to strategic client issues, disagreements may arise with clients that are more tactical or short-term in nature. Perhaps the relationship overall is good, but you are put in a position of having to tell a client "no." This is almost inevitable in any client relationship. Part of the responsibility of an excellent client manager is to **guide the client to the intersection of your organization's capabilities and their needs.** Sometimes, those needs are outside of what your organization is capable of accomplishing (or outside of your desire to invest). Or perhaps you do not need to tell the client no, but instead guide them to a mutually agreeable solution.

Fred once worked with a software company that was in the running to land a major deal. The contract was to replace the payment system of one of the largest fast-food operators in the world. The deal was enormous, with full involvement of the entire executive team and board of directors. Suffice it to say the deal was a game-changer for the entire organization.

Unfortunately, Fred and the client could not reconcile on pricing. The potential client continued to compress margins in every negotiation, and eventually, Fred realized his company would accept the business at a loss. The team re-approached the client and let them know that they really wanted to work with them (a definite yes) but could not accept the terms. Fred's team communicated in a positive, enabling way that they wished the client well in their sourcing efforts.

The client was shocked (no vendor ever said no to their organization). But because the team had negotiated in good faith (and offered a lot of "yes" along the way), the client realized that the spirit of the disagreement came from a place of trying to find a mutually agreeable solution. Eventually, they agreed to the terms. Fred's team had reserved the "no" for when it really mattered, and it made all the difference when it was needed most.

Our first recommendation for accomplishing this successfully is **don't just say no**. In the first interaction that may require disagreement, focus instead on listening and understanding. There will be time later to guide the client; avoid doing so during the initial introduction of an idea, when the client is excited.

John remembers an experience when he had recently taken over client management for a large client that used his company's technology services extensively. The client had acquired another large enterprise and commenced with technology integration, which required John's participation. The project kicked off with an overview session in a large room at the client site with dozens of participants: technology and business teams from across both enterprises, multiple vendors and consultants. The project leads walked the entire audience through the details of the integration – a colossal amount of work in a very compressed time frame. At some point during the meeting, John raised his hand and indicated that what they were proposing was not possible given the amount of work and time constraints.

To say he got a lot of feedback on that comment would be an understatement. Even people who reported to John told him it was a boneheaded statement. And they were right! John was correct on the merits, but it would have been far wiser to raise those issues later (and in a smaller forum). Of course, the project scope and time scale both changed later, but the damage was still there.

In that instance, John made the classic client manager mistake of trying to "kill a stupid idea early." Being right had nothing to do with it — what he showed the team was that he was not willing to listen. Pay close attention: The perception was 100% counter to what actually happened. John did listen, but his response is what created the perception (which became the reality) that he wasn't listening. We once had a mentor who emphasized "reality always wins" — sometimes it is better to let reality drive your intended result than announce early that you are closed-minded. This is even more true when your client's idea is not possible on merits alone. The more unlikely an idea is, the more likely your client will be emotionally wedded to it — so don't just say no.

Slow Roll the No

This idea is closely related to "Don't just say no." Sometimes, it is better to not address a disagreement directly, particularly if you are in a situation where reality always wins. Although we would generally advocate for being direct and forthright with clients, there are ways to manage disagreement so that it is not sharp and does not subtract from the relationship bank account.

We find this to be particularly helpful for requests that your organization cannot deliver on immediately. For example, perhaps a client requests a new feature or new product, and you know your company will not deliver anytime soon. Rather than responding with a hard "we can't do that," take an approach that indicates listening and relationship building. That approach might sound more like, "We don't have that today, but let us take that back to the team and get back to you with an approach." Or, "We've been thinking about that as well. We don't have it today, but we'll commit to revisiting the issue after phase three of the project." Lastly, confirming that the idea is valid or interesting but that you need some time to think through the nuances is very powerful: "That is an interesting idea. Let me think that through and run it by the team."

Persevere Until You Prevail, or Have One More Meeting

Another technique for managing client disagreement is just old-fashioned persistence! Often, clients ask for something not because it is a fundamental business need but rather because it is interesting, they have a short-term business opportunity, or they read an article about it. In other words, the request is not strategic in any way. In these cases, sometimes just talking enough about the idea can lead the client to their own conclusion that the request is too complex or impractical in the real world. The temptation for a new client manager is to try to manage the client to "make these meetings go away," particularly if others in the organization are involved. Your peers would like to spend less time on something they fundamentally believe won't work.

Try taking the opposite approach. Rather than trying to shut down the client, be willing to invest the time in exploring the area of disagreement thoroughly. As we like to say, be willing to have one more meeting than they are. By being willing to lead the next discussion at the end of the current one, you may just lead the client to the conclusion that it's time to move on!

Manage Your Own Thinking

We once had a coworker who was Ivy League educated for both his undergraduate and graduate degrees. He was one of the smartest people we have ever met, the smartest person in any room, and he needed everyone to know it. The company tasked him to work with the client very closely to conduct joint marketing of the product.

If you know anything about marketing, you know it is a field of wonderful possibilities, but great marketers often clash about the "right" way to go about it. Ivy League was of the opinion that the client was "stupid" because they would not approach the problem with the same logical process he proposed. His inability to concede to someone else's ideas resulted in an escalated phone call to our client management team: an expletive-laced tirade stating that "under no uncertain terms will we ever work with him again!" Ivy League never said anything demeaning to the client, but the client intuitively grasped the implicit criticism of their intellect.

The single largest mistake client managers often make in managing clients is not managing their own thinking about disagreement. Often, the disagreement will cause the client manager to view the client negatively on a personal level. "Can you believe how stupid these guys are?" or "I can't believe what Bill said in that meeting. He's such an idiot." We all have those feelings sometimes about our clients – it is difficult to work around that part of human nature.

Consider though: What if your client knew what you said behind closed doors? We find that clients are often much more perceptive about your feelings about them than you would ever give them credit. They may not know exactly what you say about them when they're not around, but they will almost invariably pick up on subtle cues and make judgments about your trustworthiness based on those hints.

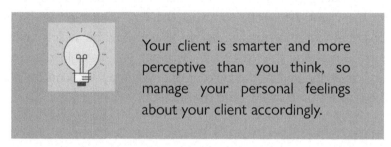

Your client is smarter and more perceptive than you think, so manage your personal feelings about your client accordingly.

We cannot emphasize enough how damaging this kind of behavior can be to any client relationship. In fact, this manifests itself even more often in senior-to-senior client relationships. Senior executives are often very intelligent, as you would expect. They tend to feel they are the "smarter" party in the relationship, particularly if they view the client as a competitor or adversary in contract negotiations. What they do not realize is that the other party often quite clearly perceives their counterpart's views, leading to a negative relationship bank account and lack of trust.

As a realistic matter, we know it is not likely you will equally respect everyone you work with in a client relationship. In truth, there are some people who are less intelligent, honest, and hard-working than others. Your client will have all types of people, and it is always true that you do not get to pick your counterparts at a client's company. There will be some people with your client who will be less important to your objectives. The fundamental question you need to ask yourself is: "Is this particular relationship important to our success?" If the answer is yes, then you must manage your own thinking.

One final note on managing your own thinking about a client's personal attributes: **Never put negative personal information about an individual client in writing.** We all have moments of frustration with other personalities, but venting in an email is not the way to manage your own emotions. There are many reasons for this hard-and-fast rule:

1. Venting about a particular client in email, interoffice chat, CRM, etc., is a permanent record of your lack of professionalism.

2. It solidifies in others the idea that it is perfectly acceptable to avoid managing their thinking about the client – and invites more of the risks mentioned above.

3. Most importantly, putting your personal feelings in writing **creates the possibility that it can be forwarded to the client.** This may sound far-fetched, but we have seen it happen. And when it happens, it is catastrophic to the relationship.

A few years ago, a client manager who worked for us completed a client call on his cell phone. He then proceeded to begin to coordinate with other members of the team to execute the client's request. He verbally told the team, "The client is really crazy on this one," and "This is dumb, but we have to do it."

Unknown to him at the time was that the cell phone in his pocket had redialed the client in question, who overheard the entire exchange, requiring considerable damage control from senior management.

In this case, the communication was not written, yet still managed to reach the client. Manage your own thinking about a client, and you will never have to face this situation.

Admit Mistakes Quickly

What if the negative interaction is not from the client, but rather because of an issue from your company? What if your company is at fault and created the issue?

The solution is simple: **Admit mistakes quickly to inoculate yourself and promote service recovery.** In the short term, admitting mistakes is a debit to the relationship account.

Interestingly, in the long term, it is massively net positive. Consumer research consistently shows that customer satisfaction scores can actually increase after a service failure, but only if the vendor follows up and resolves the issue with speed and care. In service businesses, this is called service recovery. In business, no one expects absolute perfection, and being willing to admit a mistake, explain the mistake, and resolve quickly is key to managing a relationship.

We once managed a relationship with a very large client that believed in a significant amount of operational process. We were subject to quarterly scorecard key performance indicators (KPIs), many of which were impossible to attain. Rather than pushing back, we decided to admit that we were not meeting the target and engage on the topic more often. In an effort to show our sincere desire to achieve the necessary results, we proposed a monthly review. In each meeting, we provided detailed steps to mitigate our shortfall. Our willingness to have the conversation frequently and provide transparency was enough to quiet the conversation and avoid escalation. Because of our willingness to accept responsibility and admit fault, the client viewed us as a valued partner and even recommended us to other potential clients – even though the stats told a different story. Apologizing and taking ownership are very powerful tools.

One question we often get is whether as a client manager you are empowered to apologize on behalf of your company. The answer is yes! (If you work for a company where this is not true, then there may be other issues.) Apologizing is something we do in all of our other relationships; therefore as a B2B client manager, we can utilize apologies as part of our toolkit.

Avoid Micro-Communication Mistakes

Often when communicating with a client, we make micro-communication mistakes that accidentally subtract from the relationship bank account. These are small word choices and phrases that most people use when communicating disagreement, but they unnecessarily create negativity.

AND not BUT; ALSO not HOWEVER

Read this sentence and ask if it accomplished its objective:

"Thank you for paying your invoice, but
there were several discrepancies that need
accounting attention."

Was that meant to be a thank you? Or to address the discrepancies? The sentence accomplished neither because of the "but." Similarly, consider this communication on a conference call:

"Your work to set up the production
environment was appreciated. However, you
need to upgrade the software to current
specification."

The "appreciation" was completely negated by the "however." Relationship bank accounts in both cases just took a micro-debit. Instead, use AND and ALSO to be additive when managing disagreements or issues:

- "Thank you for paying your invoice. And later we can work out some of the discrepancies."
- "Your work to set up the production environment was appreciated. Also, we'll need to upgrade the software to current specification."

Avoid the R word

This technique applies a bit more to industries with high fixed costs and output that is limited by human capital – consulting, software development, and marketing agencies. In those instances, productivity is mostly a factor of managing people and their level of output. Often, clients will ask for more work or better products, and the client manager will defend the current level of service by citing a "lack of **resources**" (the R word). This is frustrating to clients. Avoid the dreaded R word by offering up other alternatives, such as timeline planning or proposals to hire additional resources. A "no" based on resources will ultimately not satisfy a client request.

We once had a client email the director of the IT department directly about getting a minor production support issue resolved.

The IT director very innocently replied that we were strapped for resources and that it would likely be a couple of days before we could address the issue. Unfortunately, the email was quickly escalated with the client, which in turn made its way back over to our company and all the way to the desk of the CEO. As you can imagine, this did not reflect well on the director of IT and resulted in considerable work for the client management team. Do not underestimate the destructive power of the R word!

Start with the positive

When we communicate a no or disagreement to a client, we are often so concerned with delivering the message, we fail to create the right micro-communications to minimize the relationship withdrawal. A subtle reframing can make a tremendous difference in how a message is perceived. Consider some examples:

- State what to do – not what to avoid
  - "Always place orders within two days."
  - **Not:** "Never take more than two days to place an order."
- Say what you can do – not what you can't do
  - "We can meet first thing on Monday morning."
  - **Not:** "We can't meet now. It has to wait until Monday morning."
- Use neutral rather than blaming language
  - "Let me clarify what I meant."
  - **Not:** "You misunderstood what I said."
- Use words that create a positive feeling
  - "At this company, we value natural resources."
  - **Not:** "At this company, we don't waste natural resources."
- Take every opportunity to communicate positively
  - "Thank you for your email."
  - **Not:** "We have received your email."

Avoid the "again"

Often, if you are "slow-rolling the no" or "avoiding just saying no," you might have to repeat a point several times to allow it to sink in. This is a perfectly acceptable communication technique, particularly if you are patient and persistent.

Just be sure to avoid the "again" preface to your message because it sends a signal that it is somehow not worth your time to repeat yourself or implies frustration that the client is not listening to you.

Consider the difference:

- "Again, we're not going to be able to deliver the product by Friday, the earliest we can do is Monday."
- **Or,** "We can deliver on Monday. I know you'd like Friday, and we'll do our best to meet that deadline."

In that last example, we removed the "again" and reframed it to start with the positive. Double win!

Reframe the Discussion

All of us have been in conversations that start with mild disagreement and eventually spiral down until both parties are obstinate in their views. We are working hard to get to an agreement but can be unaware of the damage we are doing to the relationship.

In these situations, think of reframing the discussion by asking a question – preferably one that gets at the root cause of your client's position. It might sound something like, "It sounds like you really need this product feature at a low price. Can you tell me more about the economics of your business?" Or "I understand you are looking for delivery by Wednesday. Can you help me understand the downstream implications?"

By asking questions, not only can we pull up from the downward spiral, we can hopefully uncover additional information that may lead to creative solutions. Or the client may start to draw a different conclusion by talking it through!

Feel, felt, found

This is a classic objection-handling technique that can be useful if you are absolutely stuck for words in a disagreement. It can also sound very canned (and is also well-known enough that the other party might be aware of your technique, and therefore find it disingenuous). It sounds something like, "I understand you feel that our pricing is higher than the industry standard. We've had several customers who told us they felt that way as well. They have found that the difference is made up in quality because our uptime is 30% more than our competitors."

The important component of this technique is the **feel** – if your client believes you truly do not understand the area of disagreement, it can sound forced. One way to avoid this trap is to use this as a framework for a conversation (rather than the exact words as in the above example): First make the client understand you hear them, validate their concerns, and explain that they may find that your way of thinking has validity as well.

The balcony technique

Another classic tactic for managing negative interactions is the balcony technique. This is particularly useful if a client is emotional in an unproductive fashion. If you are new to client management, this can be a scary and unexpected development – and it can cause you to freeze. You begin taking the issue personally, which limits your ability to think and respond appropriately.

When this happens, go to the balcony: Pretend you are on a balcony overlooking this scene as though it were a play. Even give the play a name like "Business people arguing over contract language details." Remember that you cannot control anyone else's behavior – only your own. By being "on the balcony," you buy yourself time to think and respond with logic rather than emotion. It's an excellent opportunity to **concentrate on the material issues, not the small stuff.** On some level, imagining a balcony is a way to disengage from the conversation in front of you and re-engage with some of the techniques for managing disagreement.

Show Enthusiasm When You Do Agree

One final technique for managing disagreement is to adjust your behavior when you do agree. If you are truly committed to reaching a 7:1 deposit ratio, then leverage times when you and your client are in sync to make those deposits. When they bring you ideas that you are capable of executing, then communicate that you appreciate their suggestions.

It might sound something like: "Hey Phil, I really like that idea. We're going to start some mockups of the website this week and should have something ready by the end of next week. Excited to get started!" Or: "Your new marketing program is brilliant, and I think we'll move a lot of units. We'll make sure production gets ramped up on our end."

Obviously, we would never advocate being insincere. If you actually are pleased to do the work your client is requesting, then validating their work with a touch of enthusiasm can go a long way to making deposits. It will also pay dividends because when you do have to disagree, the client knows you are doing so because of a business need, not because you are disagreeable. Enthusiasm generates relationship deposits that are durable!

Tactics

1 Take greater ownership. If faced with negative relationship equity, there is always hope. Remember: "Do what you can, with what you have, where you are, right now."

2 Get to the root cause. The more forceful the "no," the more likely the other party is responding to an incentive in their organization that they do not control.

3 Don't just say no. Guide the client to a mutually agreeable solution.

4 Manage your own thinking. Clients are often much more perceptive about your feelings about them than you would ever give them credit.

5 Admit mistakes quickly. In the short term, admitting mistakes is a debit to the relationship account, but in the long term, it is massively net positive.

6 Avoid micro-communication mistakes. Small word choices and phrases most people use when communicating disagreement create unnecessary negativity.

7 Reframe the discussion. Asking questions can help you pull up from a downward spiral and get to the root cause, but it may also help the client by talking it through.

8 Be enthusiastic and sincere about agreement. This can go toward relationship deposits, but also shows that when you have to disagree, it's because of a business need.

Job #2:
Build Success
for Your
Company

Chapter 4:
Think About Growth

In the early days in our client management careers, we managed a large, unruly client that often "demanded" extra work as part of the overall relationship. Because the client was large and often unhappy with the relationship, the former client manager had routinely caved to these requests. Not only was this additional work without compensation, but it also created great stress on the organization because the work was unfunded – and performed only begrudgingly by the extended team. Most of the deliveries of the various extra items were suboptimal and completed below the client's expectations.

We simply asked the question: Why are we not charging for this work? Leveraging the skills we'll discuss in this chapter and the next (namely, project management and negotiations), we began the challenging work of proposing that all additional requests be funded by the client. Merely by enforcing this discipline, we created an annual $7 million revenue stream from almost nothing. Surprisingly, it had a secondary benefit – the broader team approached the work in a much more organized, disciplined fashion. The various projects became much more likely to be delivered on time, pleasing the client. Ironically, by doing the hard thing (asking to be paid) we actually improved the client relationship and generated fantastic growth to boot.

When thinking about revenue growth with a client, most client managers instinctively think about selling new products, projects, or services. Their path to growth lies in "selling" something new to the client.

That is an element of the role, however, the client manager is in a unique position to capitalize on opportunities that are not obvious to someone with a more casual relationship with the client. Louis Pasteur observed, "Chance favors the prepared mind." This chapter is about knowing the tools you will need to have that prepared mind, and thus be able to take advantage of opportunities to grow that others will miss.

Consider Types of Growth Beyond Revenue

In a previous role with a software startup, we started the company with a single product. We were tasked with growth in the form of channel adoption for greater reach as well as software upgrades for the purpose of efficiency. While we didn't have more products to sell, we could still have a major impact on revenue. It is the job of the client manager to help identify and drive growth opportunities regardless of how they are defined. Good times (and bad) will come and go, but an increase to the recurring revenue stream will always show up as a positive in your annual review.

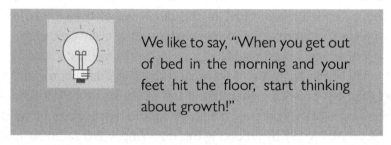

We like to say, "When you get out of bed in the morning and your feet hit the floor, start thinking about growth!"

As a client manager, your #2 job is growth. Usually, this takes the form of revenue growth (and we know that is what your executive team wants). While pressure from the executive team is focused on internal goals, rest assured the client is yearning for that same growth as well. Typically, that growth comes in the form of more existing products or services, new products, or better pricing. Sometimes, there are circumstances where revenue growth is not possible, and in that case, other types of growth may become more important. For example, there may be legal or industry reasons you cannot generate more revenue with a given client. Or your company is at capacity and cannot service any more business. In any case, as the client manager, it is incumbent on you to find ways to grow or deepen the relationship regardless of the exact nature of growth. For example, you can always deepen the number of relationships you have at the client company. Or you can find ways to improve your current service delivery and make it that much more difficult for your client to find an equal provider.

Project Management

Project management has advanced considerably as a discipline in the last two decades. Today, it is regarded as its own profession, with college courses, seminars, and dozens of books. In our opinion, much of this makes project management seem overly complex. Nevertheless, it is an important component of managing any project-based business. The good news is that with a few simple concepts, almost anyone can be a very basic project manager – including you.

There will be times your client will ask for major resources from your organization in order to grow. Since you are a growth-oriented client manager (and you thought about growth when you got out of bed), you want to execute against the request. Know when you need to leverage the tools of professional project management, and if needed, ask for help.

Rule of thumb: If a client request results in required action from three or more people, it may be time to consider the task a project. Why three or more? Because that is the limit of the number of people you can successfully monitor and still accomplish the everyday tasks of client management.

You may work in an organization without resources like professional project managers (a small company, a startup, or a business that is not project-focused), and thus need to be the project manager yourself. If so, focus on managing the four basics of project management:

- **Scope** – Define the project so everyone understands the objective
- **Resources** – What people or assets will be involved

- **Time** – The amount of time to complete the project, and creation of a project schedule
- **Money** (sometimes) – How much money you have to spend on the project (you may not manage this aspect if the project is small-scale or not resource-intensive)

At this point, we would recommend acquiring an online tool to help define the above, in particular the project plan or project steps. We've listed several excellent free (or low-cost) tools in the **Resources**.

Once you have defined the basics above in a project scope document, the rest of project management is relatively simple: tracking WHO, will do WHAT, by WHEN – and holding others accountable to complete their part of the project. The good news is that as the client manager, you are naturally in a position of authority to drive execution for your client. Project managers are a useful (and necessary) addition to any large project, but no one will care more about the outcome with your client than you will.

So, when needed, be the project manager and get that client to grow!

Goal Setting

The best client managers know the power of goal setting. Increased performance from setting goals is well researched – as recently as 2015, a study showed people who wrote down their goals were 33% more likely to achieve those goals.

If your company encourages or has an existing process for goal setting, great! Leverage their system to center your goal set on your

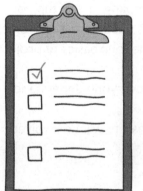

clients and their objectives. If not, create your own goal set to ensure your continued **focus on the material issues, not the small stuff**.

Try to set annual and quarterly goals for each of your clients. In addition (and perhaps more importantly) we are fans of the OKR format for goal attainment. OKR stands for Objectives and Key Results, a format pioneered by Silicon Valley tech companies like Google. The format is relatively simple: The Objective is the goal, and the Key Results are measurable metrics to determine whether you succeeded at your goal. Completing them quarterly enables better real-time feedback about whether you are achieving your objectives.

We like this format because it is easy to understand and implement – for a quarterly goal you could complete each task in less than an hour. At the end of each quarter, you can review whether you met your goals and potential areas to improve.

Another tactic to make your goals work for you is making your goals readily visible in whatever format works best for you – written on a whiteboard, taped to your monitor, or front-and-center on your desk. Having goals you (and others) can see will increase your likelihood of meeting those goals and demonstrate to your colleagues your seriousness about the science of client management.

Some managers (the good ones) will drive this process, reviewing your goals and helping you think through next quarter's goals. Regardless if that is the case, do not worry about whether you are "doing it right"... just do it. Set goals for your clients every quarter and watch as you magically begin to lead your peers in client growth.

Map the Organization

You have built a relationship with a client and have a deep understanding of things like their background, feelings towards your organization, and personal details. You have a growth plan in place as well. Now is the time to **expand your relationships and map the organization**.

Why map an organization? A few reasons:

- It allows you to identify influencers and other team members who may affect decisions about growth and whether to buy from your organization.
- It can help you identify new opportunities for growth within a client.
- It demonstrates mastery of a client – helpful in an account review or any situation where an executive wants to understand what's going on with this client.

A relationship map is a symbolic map of all key stakeholders in an organization. Usually, each person is a "card" with information such as:

- Role in the organization
- Goals (specifically beyond your product; this allows you to strategically position your product above those other needs or even displace other products with yours)
- Feelings about your product
- Influence on buying decisions (decision maker, primary POC, influencer, analyst, etc.)
- Information-gathering style

Generally, the map is an influence map, meaning each card is arranged with arrows to designate how each of them influences the others, leading to the primary point(s) of contact and the decision maker(s). In addition, creating a reporting hierarchy map can be helpful as well.

As you create the map, you will see the gaps in your relationship. For example, you may identify a person who is an analyst that is very influential to the ultimate decision maker, but not much is known about them. By identifying this weak spot, you can leverage the techniques discussed in Chapter 2 to build a relationship and understand their point of view. As you build out that relationship, they will reveal the next part of the relationship map that requires more detail. A good client manager is constantly expanding their network within the client.

Leverage Technology

One of the best parts of being a modern client manager is that many of the tools mentioned in this chapter can be enabled with SaaS[1] software that is easy to set up and relatively inexpensive. Product knowledge can be captured in a hyperlinked wiki. Projects can be managed with project management software with great features like checklists and timeline charting. Multiple CRM systems exist to track client management decisions and document relationship maps.

---

[1] Software as a Service

If your company employs any of these systems, you are ahead of the game. If not, you may want to consider investing in them yourself, with an important caveat: **Never invest in a system without first managing your projects the old-fashioned way** – with sticky notes, note cards, or a whiteboard. In other words, for a new client manager, spend time understanding which system works best for you and your business first in an analog way before investing in digital. By doing so you will be better able to articulate your needs when you invest in a software product.

Each of these growth techniques is easily managed without any technology at all. The right software, deployed correctly, can be an enabler to make this work easier. Complex or cumbersome software can have the opposite effect, where the client manager becomes a data entry associate rather than a client manager. Avoid this trap by always doing the work first and technology enablement later.

Does this mean I will be disintermediated by technology?

We've all seen the headlines regarding how new technologies will replace many jobs in our society and advances in artificial intelligence will create exceptional disruption. While these headlines may contain some hyperbole, they also carry some truth. It is undeniable that many industries and functions have succumbed to the lower cost of technology, but there are some functions that will never be touched. Client management will only increase in importance in the coming decades.

The reality is that people buy from other people, not machines. This will always be true and will never change. Business leaders will never outsource the core function of business decision-making to robots. Yes, the **kinds** of decisions they make may change, but the fundamental decision about whether to align with your organization or another will always come down to people making decisions with their heads and hearts. Human decisions can be informed with data, but in the end are made with emotion. The fundamental decision that another business makes to engage with you as a vendor is about trust and cannot be delegated to a machine.

This concept, called "high tech/high touch," was nicely encapsulated by John Naisbitt's almost 40-year-old futurist classic *Megatrends*. The conceptual idea is that every technological advance will necessitate a corresponding **increase** in the amount of human touch that is necessary. This may seem counterintuitive, but think about it. As personal computers permeated our lives in the '80s and '90s, what was their most essential function? Email, chat, message boards – most of the value was in increased forms of human communication. What about smartphones? Fantastic technology, but what is the primary use case? Texting, talking, social media, dating – all high-touch activities.

More technology results in people wanting to communicate with other people **more**, not less. The implication is profound for those interested in pursuing a career in client management.

Use technology for transactional questions and focus on the relationship

Technology solves the easy transactional questions, making the relationship (and therefore the client manager) even more important.

When we think about the type of work client managers were performing as little as ten years ago, much of it was manual reporting and status updates. Performance reports for clients, client status reports for internal managers, communications to clients about routine changes in the product – endless requirements for communication.

Slowly, many of these functions have been or will be automated away. Does that mean there is less of a need for the client management role? The opposite has proven true. As those less value-adding tasks melt away, your organization will want you to act as a strategic consultant to your clients and seek opportunities for the next business venture. Most businesses will use this as an opportunity to redirect resources to deepening relationships with clients. It is far easier to sell something new to an existing client than to find an entirely new client – and less costly by an order of magnitude.

There is one downside as technology advances and clients become more "self-serve" – as the client manager, the problems you face will only be the hard problems, not the ones you can solve in a few hours. Clients will reach out not because they need routine information or hands-on labor, but rather because they want your organization to solve some of their largest challenges. The role of the client manager in navigating these challenges will get larger but also more rewarding.

Tactics

1

If approaching a large, complex task with your client, think about asking your team to assign a project manager – particularly if the project is revenue-generating. If your company does not routinely employ project managers, consider hiring a contractor or part-time position. This will allow you to focus on the relationship, while the project manager focuses on individual tasks and deliverables.

2

Clear articulation of the project scope will eliminate confusion about the agreed deliverables and help identify additional revenue opportunities.

3

Grow your relationship map even when you are unsure whether the relationship will have any future benefit. Do not pass up opportunities to get to know other personnel from your client organization, even if their value to you is not immediately obvious. When your client asks, "Can I bring Carol to dinner?" the answer is always yes – giving you an excellent chance to expand your relationships with the client and potentially discovering new avenues for growth.

Chapter 5:
Say Yes

John had recently assumed client leadership with a very large, important client to his company. After about three months in the role, the client met with John's team at their offices (a bad sign) to inform them that they were thinking of leaving the relationship unless the contract was renegotiated. The scope of the contract was enormous, with hundreds of millions of dollars at stake, and a contract length of several hundred pages of detailed terms and conditions. John realized he would need to lead the negotiations but was frankly terrified.

Fortunately, he had recently completed a graduate school course on negotiations, and he used the next few weeks to assemble his team: a seasoned in-house counsel, outside counsel, his boss, finance, and operational experts from the organization. With the negotiating team in place, John felt comfortable putting his (until then) entirely theoretical knowledge to work. Because he was more recently familiar with negotiations theory, John was able to successfully leverage that knowledge with the team for goal setting, focusing on interests, etc. The rest of the team brought a wealth of knowledge about current company operations as well as real-world experience negotiating these large contracts. Together the assembled negotiations team performed extremely well and created an excellent outcome for both parties – a win-win. The key for John was realizing areas where he was weak and filling those gaps with experienced professionals.

Make the Commitment

We always like to start with the simplest and fastest way to grow your client – by saying yes when they ask to grow with you! This might seem obvious, but it's actually more difficult in practice. Usually, when clients want to grow their business with you, it also comes with some difficulty. The client may ask for new product features, new services, more resources, or some other increased commitment from your organization. Often, client managers will be reluctant to commit on behalf of their organization, for fear they may over-commit and under-deliver or that the request is in conflict with other initiatives. Perhaps the client manager may not feel authorized to make the commitment on behalf of the organization. Or, the new product request is not aligned with your company's product roadmap. In these scenarios, we recommend two possible courses of action.

Course 1: Make the commitment and live with the consequences

Depending on a variety of factors such as your seniority and position, your organization's capabilities, and the scope of the request, you may be able to make a decision yourself and commit on behalf of your organization to the client. Many new client managers are understandably reluctant to do this. You can probably go further here than you think – and you may be rewarded by doing so with a massive relationship deposit with your client. This path has more risk but also correspondingly more reward. As one excellent client manager put it: "If I'm going to be shot, it will be moving from foxhole to foxhole."

Course 2: Force the organization to make a clear decision

This is the safer path (but perhaps more work). If your customer makes a request that you know would grow the relationship (particularly in terms of revenue), then you have an obligation as a client manager to drive that decision within your organization. In other words, it is your responsibility to organize the right meetings, with the right people and the right materials, to force a clear-cut decision. That may mean corralling senior executives in a room and forcing them to make trade-offs they would rather not make. You will not always be loved for this – most executives would prefer that clients quietly grow and pay their invoices without too much fuss or bother. Nevertheless, client advocacy is central to your mission as a client manager, and you are obligated to project manage the decision on your company's behalf.

It is important to note that the second path may require more than one pass (i.e., you may have to organize more than one set of meetings to reach a clear conclusion). The first pass may only be to get your team familiar with the requirements to grow the client, and decision makers sometimes need space to contemplate the decision in between meetings.

All things being equal, as leaders of client managers we prefer those who tend to lean towards the first course. Why? Because more forward progress with clients is achieved that way, and in shorter time frames. Occasionally, it does result in over-committing for the company, which has to be managed with the client... and perhaps a relationship bank account withdrawal. Nevertheless, that is a small risk compared to the much greater risk of inaction in today's fast-paced business environment. As one client manager leader said to us, "I'd much rather use the bridle than the spurs."

At one memorable client, we were confronted with the task of "cleaning up" some of our technical infrastructure before we would be allowed to grow the relationship with new, revenue-generating features. We quickly cobbled together a plan. When the client asked what the plan was, the client manager emailed a detailed explanation spelling out the approach, timeline, and deliverables. After sending, several internal executives responded in frustration and disagreement with the course of action and the level of detail. The client manager was understandably concerned that he had overstepped his bounds. Surprisingly, within a matter of hours the client's executive sponsor responded with praise and appreciation for both the plan and the level of detail. The clarity built trust, strengthened the relationship, and cleared the way for continued growth. The client manager made a commitment (taking a risk in doing so) and it paid off handsomely.

Negotiations

Negotiation is another topic worthy of its own book (and there are many). Indeed, the scholarship on this topic is extensive. (Again, we have listed some of our favorite books and articles in the **Resources**.)

If your background is from the technical or operational side of a business prior to your role in client management, or if you are early in your career, the idea of negotiations may be intimidating. Just the word itself can evoke fear from all the times you have been on the wrong side of an expert negotiator, such as when buying a vehicle. However, if you want to grow with your client, you will need to have at least some ability to negotiate.

Fortunately, client management is an excellent on-ramp to learning the basics of negotiation – and basic negotiation skills are also a requirement for advancing in the role. Although you may not initially be negotiating hard business terms (like pricing and contracts), any client management role will likely be negotiating non-price items on an almost daily basis. Most of those interactions will be some form of negotiation.

Additionally, if you are delivering messages around value proposition, you will almost certainly be required to negotiate as well. We would propose you tackle the topic of negotiations with a two-pronged approach:

1. Develop a light expertise in negotiations with readily available learning materials.
2. Know when you need to enlist the help of others.

What do we mean by "light expertise"? We mean enough knowledge to conduct successful day-to-day negotiations in your business. Attend a class, read a book or two, or take an online seminar. Know some of the typical terms used in negotiations such as BAFO,[1] anchoring, and the reciprocity norm.

---

[1] Best and Final Offer

Tactics

1 The right customer is always right. In any B2B relationship, you must make wise choices about where to deploy your resources. Clients that are small (and will remain that way) or misaligned with your company's value proposition are not good investments for your time. If you ask, "Is this the kind of customer we want to invest in for the future?" there's a good chance you can gain agreement. If you're unsure whether you have the organizational standing to force your company to say yes, think through whether your executive team would agree this is the right customer, and proceed accordingly.

2 Hold recurring (quarterly) meetings to discuss strategic objectives for both you and the client. These meetings will quickly highlight growth opportunities or the lack thereof and validate the strength of the yes.

3 Consider a strategic counsel comprised of your most strategic clients.

4 Negotiations, like most disciplines, require exposure. Start by playing the role of copilot to get a feel for strategy and tone. Take copious notes and schedule an internal follow up to understand more about the strategies chosen. Pregame internally prior to every negotiation call to ensure alignment.

Chapter 6:
Remind the Client Why You are There

We once managed a large client delivering SaaS-based technology services. The client would often ask for extra project-based work (e.g., customizations specific to their software package). This was all fine, except whenever their team was unable to deliver on time, they would conveniently surface to the client executive team some technical issue to make it appear that the project delay was because of us, "the vendor." Therefore, the message was always that "the vendor" was constantly late with projects.

To address this, we designed a quarterly business review (QBR – more on this later) with the goal in mind to dispel this perception. We included three slides with an enormous list of all our completed projects for the past two years and whether they were completed on time. Out of 56 projects, all but one had been completed on time and with high quality. When we unveiled this at the QBR, in a room full of their executives, the senior executive turned to his product manager and said, "This can't possibly be true." She looked at him and said, "It is true." A long pause followed as that sank in. In a moment we had reinforced our value proposition and destroyed a long-standing myth.

It shouldn't be the case that you need to remind your clients of "the facts" – the hard work your company puts in every day to deliver on your value proposition. But you do – and you must do it repeatedly, at every opportunity.

Reinforce the Value Proposition

Client managers are sometimes surprised to learn that a large part of their role is selling the existing value proposition again. They may believe that their role is to "maintain" the relationship, not realizing that clients need to constantly be reminded of why you are there. Remember, your client does not know as much about your product or service as you do – that will not change, nor should it. If your client knows more about your product than you, then you are not doing your job.

One simple way to reinforce the value proposition with clients is to link any conversation about your product (even if in the middle of a conversation about needed improvements) to the existing benefits. Even if the benefit is something your competitors can do as well, merely linking the two together can solidify your client's perception of your value. You do not have to wait for something new to do a little selling. We're often surprised by how often client managers fail to take opportunities to reinforce the value of their product.

Highlight the feature, then discuss the benefit. It might sound something like: "Sounds like we need to create a new metrics dashboard for your software implementation. We'll get to work on it right away. One of the nice things about our software architecture is the ability to deliver changes very quickly."

What just happened there? We did several things at once, all in three sentences:

1. Sought to understand by reflecting back the request
2. Enthusiastically agreed to work
3. Reinforced the value proposition

 If you are ever stuck on how to communicate the value proposition, start with this improvisational phrase: "And the great thing about that is..." Your mind will fill in the rest, and you will quickly be communicating value propositions in an effortless way.

Conduct a Periodic Business Review

It is important to reinforce value propositions in a more structured format. A discipline we recommend is a periodic business review. Often these are quarterly, but depending on industry structure and size of the client, once or twice a year may make more sense. The stated purpose of the meeting with your client is to review the operations of your relationship, discuss any outstanding issues, and perhaps plan for the future. The actual reason for the meeting is the opportunity for you, as the client manager, to reinforce the value proposition of your company. To that end, try to schedule more than the usual amount of time you spend with the client. For example, if you tend to meet regularly for an hour once a month, schedule a bi-annual, two-hour business review. Position the meeting as a deep dive where both parties can spend time thinking through the relationship and potential improvements.

The agenda for your business review can vary. Collaborate with your client in advance to set the agenda for the meeting. By involving them in the process, you create more buy-in for next steps and results.

In addition, we also believe business reviews work best when you share any prepared materials in advance (at least a day or two before the meeting). This has the benefit of involving your client in the process, but more importantly, it prevents your client from being surprised by any negative information that may reflect poorly on them. Regardless, the main priority is to use the business review to reinforce your value proposition. As an added benefit, you will gain considerable insight into your client's position on the relationship, the product, and what the future state might look like from their perspective.

Typical elements of a quarterly business review

What makes for a good quarterly business review? Each one is unique, and your primary role as the client manager is to determine the most appropriate messaging for your client that reaffirms your value proposition. Having said that, here are some typical elements of a QBR:

1. **Review of current operations and performance metrics.** Remember: "What gets measured gets managed." So this is your chance to set their thinking, not just report the weather. View this as an opportunity to set the agenda for what is important. One tactical suggestion: If applicable, do not forget to include economic business metrics as well, such as revenue, costs, or margin. If your value proposition is to help another business improve their economics, then these metrics (if available and applicable) can be very appropriate discussion points.

2. **Plans for growth.** Review new products and services from your firm or potential projects that would grow your joint business. If your business depends on your client's growth, then perhaps discuss channel marketing or joint marketing efforts. Regardless, this is your opportunity to grow the client!

3. **Product roadmap or future strategy discussion.** For senior executives, this is probably their favorite part. Use this opportunity to think blue sky, brainstorm, and be big-picture. What are the business ideas your company is thinking about three to five years from now? This is your opportunity to gain strategic alignment from your clients early in that process. Your client's participation is a big statement about their commitment.

> Business reviews are not the place to highlight either party's shortcomings. Frustrations should be addressed with a smaller audience in a thoughtful manner.

Be the Master of Your Products and Services

As a client manager, you are in a unique position to bridge the gap between strategic selling and on-the-ground operations. Often, you will find yourself in a position where the sales team has oversold the capabilities of your organization. This is not necessarily a bad thing! The role of any good sales organization is to link the potential client's strategy to the capabilities of your organization. In that process, the exact nature of your product or service can get lost.

The way to bridge this gap is to get physical with your product, preferably by using it yourself as a customer, and become an expert in it. You are responsible for the next level of detail – being able to work with the client to match your existing capabilities to their needs. For example, if your company sells heavy construction equipment, you need to be able to articulate the value of the product as a user would, and the best way to do that would be to learn to operate the equipment yourself. You do not need to be an expert operator or a mechanical engineer, but you do need to be able to convey what a user experiences and how that is a value proposition to your client. Your product knowledge must be more in-depth than a salesperson, who focuses more on their knowledge of the marketplace, pricing, contracts, etc.

If you sell software, be a regular user of that software. If you distribute retail merchandise, be a user of the most important items in your inventory. (These are tax-deductible business expenses in the US.) In other words, become an enthusiast of your product, and the value propositions will come naturally to you.

We recognize this may be difficult for some industries, particularly commodities. If you work for a gasoline refinery, it would be hard to articulate the joy of gasoline. However, it is always possible to experience the product from the customer's point of view: Perhaps ride along for a gas delivery or spend time in manufacturing to understand the process to consistently deliver high quality. There is always a way to get physical with the product.

The Power of Story

Any experienced salesperson will tell you that good selling is actually good storytelling. All of the data, statistics, and charts in a typical business presentation are next to useless compared to its impact on the human psyche. Storytelling creates real human connections. The art and science of communicating a strong narrative in sales is well worth its own book, and we won't cover that here (we have listed various high-quality reads in the **Resources** to take your knowledge to the next level).

A typical story in a sales presentation is almost a three-act play where the client (or someone like the client) is the hero of the story. Act one is usually a problem description, or perhaps "Why our company was founded." Act two is the complication: "Why the problem won't go away, how it's getting worse, how nobody has solved it before," etc. Act three is the resolution: "How our product solved the problem, created a hero within their company, and how it will do the same for you." Roll credits.

However, you may not have the opportunity or even the need to develop a full story around your product or service, as this is typically within the purview of a sales-oriented role. As a client manager, you are often leading meetings dealing with operational issues or quarterly business reviews – formats that do not naturally lend themselves to great storytelling.

Is there a role for story in client management?

Absolutely! We recommend always having three to five quick stories available about how your clients used the product, a feature, or a service from your organization to become the hero. These stories can be about almost anything, as long as you can link the part of your business under discussion to a story about client success. More often than not, a peer who has been in the role longer can be a great resource for such stories.

We'll often (anonymously) discuss how other clients are leveraging our product and how you, Client B, can and should do the same. The result is that the Client B product owner can increase advocacy for the product, help others achieve their objectives, and drive further usage of the product within their organization. These illustrations of value are priceless because that product manager has taken a risk to adopt your product.

You do not have to be a master of sales to create great stories for your clients. Think of it more like a story you would tell your friends. Even if you are not a natural storyteller, being able to relate the experiences of other clients is a natural client management skill.

Tactics

1

Claim victory at least once during any meeting with a client. Even if the meeting is about the seven things your company has failed to deliver, invent or add an eighth item that is a positive message of something you achieved for the client. Look for a trend within those seven items that highlights improvement. Know the root cause of those failures to ensure a clear understanding among all parties. Be prepared to defend your organization without being defensive.

2

As client managers, we tend to focus on what's wrong – all of the issues in the relationship. Even when your relationship bank account is depleted, and your client lets you know it on a daily basis, do not allow yourself to be overwhelmed. It is your responsibility to display resilience and composure in front of your team at every client meeting as well as reinforce whatever value proposition still exists for your company.

3

Become your client's consultant by mastering your product and the competitive landscape – get hands-on with what you sell, and be aware of emerging trends.

Chapter 7:
Lead by Example

While working for a very small startup, John was tasked with managing their biggest client — one of the largest companies in the world. The stakes were high.

The client demanded a monthly deep dive of all financials and key performance indicators (KPIs). The nature of the request, combined with a lack of experience from most of the participants, made everyone anxious. John quickly realized how important it was for him to diffuse tension, set the tone, and put everyone at ease.

John identified the exact client requirements and asked the team to prepare rigorously. Before each meeting, he led multiple internal reviews to ensure everyone was on-message. Most importantly, John kept a calm demeanor regardless of the tone of the meeting. After the third meeting, the VP of Finance looked at John and said, "I can't tell you how glad I am that you are running this account. When this meeting first came up, I thought it would be death by firing squad every month, but you somehow manage to keep them calm even when we have a bad month."

John knew his job went well beyond maintaining relationships or reporting revenue — his real job was leadership for the organization.

Bring Order from Chaos

We often encounter client managers who are at wit's end — they want what is best for their clients and for the company, and yet they feel unsupported. The call center team makes mistakes, the products do not ship on time, documentation is nonexistent, or executives do not seem to care about the clients. We have seen all these things before — and we have been there ourselves.

As a client manager, it is unlikely you can solve all these issues yourself, particularly in a large organization, but you have a responsibility beyond the client to provide leadership for your entire organization. You have a special and unique responsibility as the voice of the customer to create as much organization as you can from the chaos. We once had an account team leader who liked to say, "Do not wait for headquarters to solve your problems." In other words, do what you can, with what you have, where you are, right now. Bring organization out of chaos.

In this chapter, we discuss some techniques you can execute today to provide greater leadership for your organization. As you become a more disciplined client manager, your internal team will respond more to your leadership – and will deliver more for your clients.

Know Your Numbers

Being the organized, driving client manager for your organization starts with the simple maxim: "Know your business." All organizations and relationships have KPIs. We recommend that you know three to five of the top performance indicators for your major clients from memory. Client managers should have a strong command of their clients' performance and be capable of stepping into any meeting with an understanding of the data, trends, and reason for any deviation. You will have three possible constituents for this information: executives, clients, and seagulls. More on seagulls in a bit!

Your executive team will look to you to be the expert. They are usually keenly aware of the macro trends but are probably not aware of the performance data at a client level. Knowing the same data points at a client level proves that you are the true business owner of the client. In addition, being regarded as a numbers person is good for your career – particularly in front of the financially-oriented executive. Having a firm grasp of the accounting rules that govern your business doesn't hurt either (as your career progresses, you will need to acquire finance knowledge anyway – so start now).

Clients will also benefit from your knowledge of their performance indicators. Being able to immediately recall this information will enable you to reinforce your value proposition, as it demonstrates you know their business.

What is a seagull? It is anyone who swoops into a client situation, poops all over everything, and swoops out! Many executives pressed for time who are unfamiliar with your client will be seagulls. Knowing the health of your business will enable you to refute a seagull who cherry-picks one issue with the client to suggest poor performance on your part. Knowing your numbers enables you to defend your work with your client.

Set Up Recurring Routines

We know many client managers who think to themselves, "I'm here to manage the relationship, so I'll take things as they come." Certainly, good client managers act with urgency in real time when necessary. But truly great client managers plan ahead and commit to a time-based discipline of weekly, quarterly, and annual events on their calendars to ensure they are driving the agenda for their clients.

The calendar for these events can vary somewhat based on factors such as the size of the client, the tenure of the client, and their health/performance. For example, you may not do a full quarterly business review for a very small client, but rather reserve that level of effort for an annual review. Most importantly, understanding what your (internal and external) clients want will drive your schedule.

Your company's structure and products may also dictate the schedule. We would suggest always scheduling major milestone events, such as:

- "Know your numbers" review
- Business reviews with the client
- Short updates
- Product updates – includes any changes to your current product's infrastructure or efficiency
- Financial review

Your calendar might look something like this:

Deliverable	Frequency	Reason
"Know my numbers" – review top 3 client stats for my top 10 clients	Weekly	Company is growing quickly, and operational metrics may change
Brief "ping" update – 5 bullets plus 1 data chart with the health of the business for my #1 client	Monthly	The client asked in our last meeting to get a brief monthly update
Full Business Review – 10-page presentation delivered in-person at the client's office for my top 3 clients	Quarterly	The most strategic clients that I need to hit my yearly growth targets
Product roadmap update in an email to all my clients	Quarterly	Ensure all clients understand our product roadmap
Account Review/ Update	Quarterly	Be ready for an account discussion at any time
Strategy review with the client's executive team	Annual	Drive our value proposition with their executive team

A regularly scheduled Business Review is the best way to ensure you have a strong command of your client's performance. The frequency may vary. For example, if the client has a negative relationship bank account, you may consider doing this more frequently.

Fred once had a client in a bad state, and his team committed to a monthly business review. It was an enormous effort, requiring dozens of hours of analysis and the preparation of a 20-page briefing. Given the frequency, they didn't deliver this personally but over email and followed with a brief conference call to answer questions. This was successful in circumventing a regular thrashing because Fred's team was proactively communicating, and it helped to avoid surprises. In general, most of Fred's clients have been happy with quarterly reviews and a small handful with an annual review.

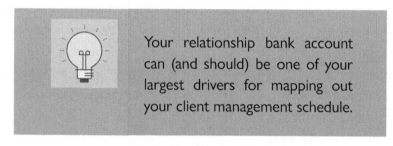

Your relationship bank account can (and should) be one of your largest drivers for mapping out your client management schedule.

Be ready for an account review

The dreaded account review – if your company makes a routine practice of them, that's excellent! (Although you may not feel that way if it involves extensive documentation.) But if account reviews are not common, we recommend that you remain ready for one at any time.

What is an account review? Every company does it differently (and many do not do it at all). The usual format is one to two pages of slides (or the readout from a CRM product) with the status of the account and relevant metrics, performed quarterly or semi-annually. Often the review may be led by sales and be more heavily focused on the sales pipeline within the client. Many times, the account review is performed with executive leadership, making it a nerve-wracking event for a newer client manager. Client managers are often not aware that the review is used by senior leaders to evaluate the talent level of their client staff. No pressure!

Regardless of whether your company performs account reviews, aim to be almost ready to have one at any time, with a few hours' notice. Keeping your account review updated will enable you to have a structured conversation at a moment's notice with teammates or your boss. It will also elevate your thinking about strategies to deepen the relationship (relationship mapping) and ideas for increased growth. If your company is smaller and does not have an established account review, refer to the **Resources** for a suggested template.

The content will vary based on your business. However, we suggest a general framework around:
1. Deepening the relationship
2. Growing the relationship
3. Everything else

Manage the Executive Team

One of the most challenging aspects of managing any client is managing your own internal executive team. Many executives enjoy client interaction and want to assist you in growing your client base. Others do not have this inclination and have to be dragged to client meetings where they have a role. Still others think they are valuable in client interactions, but they are actually not helpful.

Regardless of your situation, understand that **a client manager must be the leader in any regard with the client, even up to the level of directing your executive team**. You are the person most familiar with the client. You are the central node for anything that happens with the client, good or bad.

Our favorite analogy is that client management is a basketball team. You are the team captain, but anyone can take shots on the goal. Your role is to ensure everyone stays coordinated as a team, and sometimes that means you provide direction to teammates more senior (and maybe even more skilled) than you. Certainly, more senior business leaders may overrule you on a client management issue, but until that happens, assume you are in charge. Too often we see client managers who bring a senior leader to the client and then relax so the senior leader can "do their thing." The more appropriate posture is to assume you are the leader until otherwise obvious.

You may be lucky and work with senior leaders who are skilled client managers and additive to any client interaction. If so, you are fortunate and should use those resources well. Unfortunately, that will not always be the case. In these situations, we have the following recommendations.

Make it easy for your executive team

If your executive teammate is reluctant to participate in client interactions but necessary for a particular function, think through ways to make their role easier. For example, if you need them to communicate a particular message, you could draft a well-crafted email and give it to them as a template. Or instead of dragging the executive to an in-person meeting, you can have the executive participate via phone while you attend the meeting in person. For a negotiation, it might mean negotiating everything else ahead of the one area where the executive needs to take the lead. Not every executive wants client interaction. In these cases, ask for something specific from your executive. While this is unfortunate, your best bet is to manage the situation to get the leverage you need from them but not expect much more.

Minimize their time spent communicating with the client

For the executive who is willing but unskilled, minimize their time spent communicating with your client. If the executive offers to create a presentation or send an email, suggest that you take the lead and escalate to them later if different results are needed. Your executive in this case should understand they are best used only for non-routine matters. If they are too far down in the weeds, it impairs their efficiency. However, there will be times where you will not be able to convince them of this point of view. If they cause relationship damage (in an email, meeting, or any other format), follow up in a way to make some relationship deposits. Your responsibility is to ensure you minimize relationship debits with your client — not "fix" your executive. As a practical matter, it is unlikely your feedback to your executive would be well received. Therefore, your best bet is to mitigate the damage and minimize the exposure as much as possible.

John once worked for an executive who was absolutely dreadful in client situations. He believed he was smarter than everyone, particularly clients. He always made sure to do more talking than listening in client meetings, and often in an argumentative way. Immediately after leaving every meeting, he would come back to the office and tell everyone how stupid that particular client was. Of course, this was not helpful, and more junior associates would pick up on this behavior and think it was acceptable. He had never led any type of client management function previously and therefore did not give it much credit as a business discipline.

The lack of disciplined thinking showed. Behind his back, clients would come to John and complain. What the executive didn't realize is that most astute businesspeople can pick up on the subtle cues that you hold them in disregard, and they don't appreciate it. However, rather than throw him under the bus, in those situations John would help the client try to understand that the executive's intent was positive and that, of course, their organization was committed to positive relationships. John would make suggestions to try to limit the executive's exposure to clients if at all possible.

Some executives will "jump you" – in other words, communicate directly with a client and forget to inform you of the discussion, or not copy you on written communication. As long as the executive is not in the latter category from above, this is usually fine. Your goal is to be in the communication process so you can maintain your position as the central coordinator for all things concerning your client. The best way to handle this is to communicate to the executive that they are always welcome to communicate with your client – more communication is better! At the same time, respectfully remind the executive your role is to be the node for the organization with the client, and you ask that they copy you or at least keep you informed of any interactions. We find that most executives are busy and forget this important step, and they intend nothing malicious. Usually, one gentle reminder is enough.

Leadership Beyond the Executive Team

In addition to your executives, be prepared to lead the entire organization. We are not fans of matrix organizations,[1] but it can be the right framework for certain companies. We'll stick with our basketball team analogy (since that sounds more fun): You are the team captain, there to help everyone around you to score points. To that end, **you are empowered to provide direction to the team**. This does not mean that you should walk down the hall and set the prioritization for your software programmers (or others who do not report to you), but it does mean that you need to facilitate the necessary dialogue.

Soon after Fred had taken over as the client manager for his company's most important client, his first task was to run point for a very large, important meeting. The CEO (who was very client focused) asked all of the executives in the company to provide slideware and data points for the meeting. Fred was a director at the time but tasked with holding all of the executives accountable for their deliverables. Sounds easy enough, but there was one problem. None of the executives delivered by the deadline. New to the business and unsure of what to do, Fred asked his boss for guidance. His response was simple: Provide the CEO with what you have (which was basically nothing). The CEO immediately jumped into action and demanded a response from the executive team to get the deliverables done ASAP! Fred was thrilled, but in retrospect, he should have realized he was already empowered to deliver for the client. It was a great lesson for him. Had he not informed the CEO of their progress (or lack thereof), they would have stepped into that meeting ill-prepared, and it would have been on Fred's shoulders. While we should all be respectful of the chain of command, sometimes the mission should supersede.

Leading by example extends even to servant leadership. Sometimes, the little things you can do as a client manager have the most positive impact on your support team. They take their cues

---

[1] Matrix organizations are set up as a grid, or matrix, rather than a traditional hierarchy. As the matrix structure combines two or more types of organization structures, some individuals report to more than one supervisor or leader (such as a functional manager and product manager).

from you – if you lead from a place that shows you value them and their work, they will respond in kind. If you view them as a means to an end, then just the opposite will occur. Particularly when you are assisting a technical team with their work, a small demonstration of humility and appreciation can have a massive impact.

John was new to a company and coordinating his first software upgrade. He decided to go on-site with the technical team, even though he would not technically be doing anything. He went mostly to see what goes into a software upgrade and to help with communications to the client. Perhaps more importantly, he was there to fetch coffee, food, snacks, or whatever else the upgrade team needed. Clearly this was not something that he needed to do, but John wanted to show them he was part of their team – and to illustrate the important role that everyone plays when it comes to client management. The upgrade went very well, and as a thank you, he bought the technical team 50-yard line tickets to the local NFL game. As you would expect, this was a massive deposit that earned him credibility with the team. After that, his clients were always top priority with the technical team.

Lead Operators with Respect, but Not Reverence

The client manager role comes with a responsibility to lead other, more operational or technical roles. Perhaps you need to interact with the product development team or your call center. Perhaps you are on a project requiring you to work closely with a technology team. Regardless, part of your remit is the management of teams focused on delivery. They may be older and more experienced than you, which can be intimidating.

Treat senior operators with respect, and you will win the day. If you feel the need to raise your voice or resort to heavy-handed tactics, consider why a so-called client manager would do such a thing. Business is full of trade-offs, and generally the short-term gain of this type of behavior is far smaller than the long-term relationship damage.

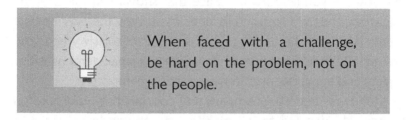

When faced with a challenge, be hard on the problem, not on the people.

For most of you, this is obvious – we know you always treat your colleagues with respect. However, we would offer one thought, particularly if you are already a respectful peer: **Your operations/ delivery team is probably capable of 30% more than you think.** Great leaders are respected because they respect everyone and the work they do. But they also always ask for more and expect excellence. Do not lower your standards because your execution team says they are too busy or "out of bandwidth." These are stock phrases meant to limit the scope of your requests. Your mandate is to build the client relationship and grow the client. Ask for 30% more than what is reasonable, and you will be rewarded with even more execution.

Fred was once asked by a very large prospective client if the company could create a wholesale change to their client services software tool. Fred asked the technical team if this was feasible, to which the answer was a clear and firm no. Fred had three choices:

1. Overrule the technical team and tell the prospective client yes, with the risk of alienating the technical team and underdelivering to the client.
2. Tell the prospect no, thereby losing the potential relationship and making the technical team happy.
3. Tactfully push the collective team to find a compromise.

Fred chose the third option and proceeded: "Team, I understand we can't commit to a complete overhaul, but please help me find a middle ground." Fred followed up on his commitment to help solve the problem by scheduling brainstorming sessions to identify other options. Fred told the prospect: "We have identified three options to address your concern. Of the three options provided, which do you think will be most effective in resolving your concern?" Naturally, the client picked an option to everyone's mutual satisfaction. Fred performed the basic client manager function of steering the potential client to a solution within the company's ability to execute. More importantly, he provided leadership by asking the technical team to deliver more than they thought themselves capable of delivering.

Lead Even When You Don't Know What You're Doing

One of our favorite movie quotes is from the first Indiana Jones movie, *Raiders of the Lost Ark*:

> **Indiana Jones:** "Be ready for me; I'm going after that truck."
>
> **Sallah:** "How?"
>
> **Indiana Jones:** "I don't know. I'm making this up as I go."

By its very nature, client management is stressful. You do not do any routine work, therefore you are constantly challenged with new situations. Surprises happen: People can be unpredictable, and business moves faster than ever. This means you will constantly be thrust into new situations without a roadmap. There is only one thing to do: **Lead even when you are not confident.** When faced with a new situation (new to you or new to the client), there is a good chance you are not the only one who lacks confidence about how to proceed. Providing leadership will ensure that you will determine a solution sooner rather than later, even if you do not know what that solution may ultimately entail. In general, action is always better than inaction, even if the action is slightly wrong.

Tactics

1 Increase your expertise about your core product. By being a product expert, you will naturally assume a leadership role in any client conversation and gain confidence.

2 Lead with respect, but avoid reverence. Great leaders are respected because they respect everyone and the work they do, but they also always expect excellence.

3 Schedule account reviews, but be ready to discuss an account at any time.

4 Be an industry expert. Client managers touch on all aspects of the business, uniquely positioning them to be subject matter experts.

Job #3: Manage Tasks and Demands That Get in the Way

Chapter 8:
Business Travel

Business travel can be one of the least considered but most challenging aspects of client management. Even the most experienced and seasoned business travelers will make mistakes.

A client manager friend told us about a mistake that nearly cost her a client. It was her first meeting after replacing an earlier client manager – an opportunity to introduce herself and set the right tone with a professional presentation. The meeting was a two-hour drive from the office – easy, no need to pack for travel. Unfortunately, she forgot the client was across a state line (in a different time zone) and arrived for the meeting an hour late to witness her boss conducting the meeting and presentation. The meeting was an A+ for content and direction… and an F for logistics. The details of business travel can make or break a client manager.

Business travel may seem like an unusual topic for a business book, but we believe doing this well leads to better client meetings and therefore better results – improved relationships and growth. As a client manager, you will be required to travel to varying degrees depending on the nature of your business, as well as the scope and location of your client base. There are a few rules to remember that will simplify the process and make it more enjoyable.

Remember: **Your number one priority of business travel is to execute the intent of your meeting for your client.** Everything else is secondary. A business trip is not a sightseeing trip. It is not for your benefit; no need to bring a swimsuit. If you treat it as work, you will execute your goals. If you view it as a vacation, not so much!

The Three Commandments of Business Travel

Neither of us are Moses, but let's start with some basic commandments (stone tablets not required).

Commandment 1: Pack light and never check a bag if flying

This may seem obvious for a business trip, but we would not list it if we had not seen this mistake with many new client managers. This should be easy unless you are traveling overseas or for an extended period (and we would argue that for even up to a two-week trip, one bag is entirely possible). Even international travel can be accomplished with one bag — it is even more important in that instance. There is almost no business trip that justifies checking a bag.

The number one reason for not checking a bag is to prevent lost luggage. Keeping the bag with you negates the risk of losing your items. If you travel for work with quick turnaround time, lost luggage is a catastrophe. A lost suitcase will not be delivered to your hotel on time, and since your business travel likely involves a meeting the next day (at the latest), you cannot afford to risk lost luggage.

Not checking a bag will also save money (which you can spend on clients), but more importantly, it will save considerable time. This makes for more amenable travel companions if traveling with peers or senior leaders. Most coworkers will probably not let on the inconvenience of waiting with you at the carousel or watching as you struggle to get your bags out of a vehicle — but they are thinking it. If you engage in enough business travel, one of your primary objectives should be to minimize the amount of time you spend in airports and maximize your time resting or being with a client. Nothing wrong with airports, but if you travel several times a month or more, this is time that could be spent working. Just because you are on the road doesn't mean the rest of your work will go away.

In a previous life, we worked for a high-ranking executive who simply would not wait at the baggage carousel with his client managers. He would say, "See you at the hotel," hop in the nearest Uber, and be gone. Knowing that you have irked your boss can be unnerving — which is the last thing you need prior to a big client meeting.

Commandment 2: Think through logistics

Focusing on logistics ensures you have plenty of time to get to your meeting destination and set expectations for others to do the same. This sounds easy enough (and like common sense) but is very often overlooked, leading to disaster. As you become a more seasoned, experienced professional, you can allot less time to get to destinations early. In the meantime, ensure you are early and that any traveling companions are as well. Items to consider in this regard include leaving for the airport in time to account for traffic, parking, and long security lines, as well as traffic at your destination. If you have a morning meeting, fly or drive in the night before. Also, make sure you know the exact location of your meeting. Do not rely solely on mapping software – give the client's executive assistant a call and confirm the exact building and room. This is also a great time to inquire about the technology available for the presentation (more on this later).

All of these suggestions may sound pedantic, but they are a serious part of excellent client management. Thinking through the logistics of a meeting and directing those around you can prevent embarrassment.

If you think directing those around you is micromanagement or should not be required, think again. One of our client managers once set up an important meeting in Seattle. The client manager followed all of the necessary steps, including ensuring the attendance of her Chief Technology Officer. On cue, the CTO showed up in the lobby of the Marriott with plenty of time to travel to the meeting. Unfortunately, he was at the Marriott in Portland. In the CTO's busy schedule (and because he did not have an assistant to track these details), he made the wrong flight arrangements.

Do not underestimate what can go wrong with logistics! Per the example above, you will need to manage peers and superiors alike.

Commandment 3: Coordinate all the necessary internal parties

You are responsible for ensuring all internal parties are aware of the meeting, know who needs to attend (both physically and virtually), and know who needs to prepare and present. It is your job to ensure everyone is making the necessary accommodations regarding flights, hotel, and attire! Depending on your organization, it may or may not be your responsibility to make everyone's travel arrangements – but at the very least, it is your role to herd the cats.

For any important client meetings requiring internal coordination, a good client manager will coordinate one or more pre-meetings with internal staff to coach their efforts. These meetings are an opportunity to provide direction to the team. For example, if one member of the team needs to create a presentation, create an outline for them and ensure they build the materials. Provide coaching on the allotted length of their presentation. Most importantly, have them practice in front of you unless you are already confident in their speaking ability. This is especially important for those who do not typically interact with clients. Back office personnel vary widely in terms of presentation creation and public speaking abilities.

Surprising to many client managers, this applies doubly to senior executives. Unless they have a pre-existing relationship with the client, an executive at your company may be less aware of the issues affecting your client than your peer team. Often, senior executives are highly willing to accept leadership from others for their actions. They want to put their best foot forward with the client just like you. If senior leadership is too busy or unavailable, we recommend preparing a pre-brief for the senior executive. This can be as simple as an email with the required talking points on their part or sharing the latest account review. Regardless of the format, the most important task is to ensure your senior leadership is pre-briefed before they walk into the meeting room. This means making sure senior leaders are keenly aware of the good, the bad, and the ugly. If a sneak attack is possible (such as the one mentioned at the beginning of the book), then set expectations. Not doing so can be limiting to your career.

Also, ensure that you level-match the participants (e.g., if your CEO will attend, ensure your client includes the appropriate counterpart). This may not necessarily mean their CEO must be in attendance (particularly if the organizations are sized differently), but you don't want your CEO meeting with an intern.

Lastly, just as you are responsible for planning the meeting, you are responsible for planning any associated client entertainment. Generally, this will be a business dinner or sometimes an event (more on this later).

Think through the reason for your meeting – if it recognizes a milestone event, make it special. If you are launching a product with a new client, plan a celebration instead of a standard business dinner. Sometimes just calling the gathering a special event name like "celebration" or "launch party" can provide shared meaning for all of the participants, even if you do not have a special venue in mind.

Dress Code

For better or worse, dressing for business now runs the gamut of style from startup casual to business formal. This makes business discussions potentially more casual, but also increases the range of potential dress code mistakes.

For a client meeting, dress one level up from your client. For example, if your client is startup casual with jeans and t-shirts, wear slacks and a collared shirt/blouse. If they are business casual, wear a sport coat/casual suit. If they wear suits, wear a suit and a tie. Good news: If your client wears full suits, you do not need to wear a tuxedo. (However, if anyone reading this book decides a tuxedo is in order, please do so and send us a video of the meeting.)

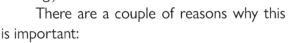

There are a couple of reasons why this is important:

1. You want to present a professional reputation for your company.
2. If your dress is significantly below your client's standard, you will be uncomfortable and mentally absent from your meeting. In many ways, the dress code is for you, not your client, because dressing appropriately allows you to ignore that part of your presence and instead focus on doing your job of delivering on your company's value proposition.

Early in John's business career, he attended his first client meeting after working in an internal role for a few months. He inquired about the dress code with one of the engineers attending the meeting (his first mistake), who encouraged John to wear what he normally wore in the office (business casual). Needless to say, John showed up to his first client meeting in a casual sweater while everyone else was wearing sport coats or suits. Being in the wrong attire caused him to lose focus entirely and reduced his effectiveness in the meeting. In fact, it is the only thing he remembers about the meeting to this day.

Tactics

1 Think like a logistics expert when scheduling business travel: It's all about the location of the event, how you get there, and what you bring.

2 Double, triple, and quadruple check your arrangements. Take responsibility for also checking the arrangements of your team.

3 Pack light and never check a bag. Not checking a bag saves time and money, and it also negates the risk of losing your luggage.

4 Strategize what to wear. Aim to be neither the most overdressed nor too casual. If you aren't sure, check the client's LinkedIn for company pictures, or simply ask.

Chapter 9:
Meetings and Agendas

We once participated in a new business pitch meeting that was in an on-site location with the client, and the plan of attack was a slideshow as well as a live technology demonstration. We planned to use a screen-share program and conference line for participants not in the room. After starting the meeting a few minutes late due to pleasantries, the salesperson tried to connect to a projector. Unfortunately, he did not have the right equipment, which started a hunt to find the correct connector. Next, he tried to set up the screen-share, only to realize the meeting was in a room without a Wi-Fi connection. Fortunately, we had a Wi-Fi hotspot that we could use... but we were in a basement that blocked the signal. Realizing we would need to send out the presentation (which would leave us without a live demonstration for those on the phone), we tried to email the slideshow to all participants. This did not work because the slideshow exceeded the allowed file size for the client. The client at that point offered us a memory stick so they could upload the file themselves, but the file size was still too large to move with the memory stick. We tried to convert the slideshow to a PDF, but of course that did not work either. We were on the verge of doing a presentation with sock puppets.

You get the idea. We started the meeting almost an hour behind schedule, at which point the VP in charge of the buying decision announced she had to leave for another meeting. The best part was on the ride back to the airport, the salesperson looked at everyone in the cab and said, "That went pretty well!" Needless to say, we didn't get the business.

Prepare, Prepare, Prepare

It may be obvious, but **your first step for any client meeting is to prepare an agenda**. Through the course of your career, you will be asked to attend meetings that vary greatly in terms of specificity. Some will be three-day design sessions that require an army of technical resources, while others will be thirty-minute sessions to "grip and grin," ending promptly in a bar. Regardless, it is your job to make sure you are absolutely clear on the purpose of the meeting. Send the agenda a day or two ahead of sending any prepared materials to gain concurrence and smoke out any hidden agenda items the client may wish to discuss.

Once the agenda is finalized, share all meeting details in an electronic calendar invite for all parties. Why is this important? Other kinds of record-keeping (particularly email) can get lost, and having elements in all different places can lead to confusion (and teammates/clients who repeatedly ask for each). Create an invite which acts as one handy reference point for all aspects of the meeting, including the agenda, logistics, materials, and conference/screen share details.

Try taking the typical preparation activities further: **Prepare something for every client meeting, even when they ask you not to prepare.** In particular, prepare something for any meeting where the agenda is not specific. Often people think of meeting preparation as slides, but we've found some of the most effective meetings are instead structured discussions with an agenda only. Regardless, your team should be mentally prepared with talking points, facts, and updates that will carry the conversation effectively.

Several years ago, we had a meeting that demonstrated this concept very well. The new executive sponsor at a key client called and asked for an on-site meeting. Eager to please the new sponsor, the client manager gladly obliged, but he failed to get the exact agenda and purpose of the meeting. We then informed one of our executives of the meeting. Unsure of the purpose of the meeting, we were not convinced it would be a good use of the executive's time. We made this clear to our executive, but he insisted that he attend. We probed our new executive sponsor on the client side for the purpose of the meeting but never did gain clarity.

We loaded the car and headed to our client's facility, with our executive in tow. Upon arrival, a member of our client's executive team pulled us aside and informed us that the sourcing team was planning to grill us on our metrics to satisfy the detractors in the audience. Thankfully, we had prepared some briefing materials. Far more importantly, we had an executive on hand who was very experienced in handling these situations. The meeting started with over a dozen of their associates pelting us with questions – versus our team of two – like a congressional inquiry. We leveraged our materials (that were somewhat related, but mostly just made us look prepared) and our executive to deflect the most obnoxious questions. The meeting turned out to be surprisingly effective, but only because we had prepared. Lessons learned:

1. Always press for an agenda.
2. Never walk into a meeting empty-handed. Always know your business and be prepared to speak to it.

Your next preparation rule is to **prepare early**. How early? It can depend a bit on the depth of the topic and the participants, but a general rule of thumb is to have an agenda solidified three days before the meeting and any written materials completed the day before. Often, meetings come together with a final agenda the day before or sometimes even mere hours before the meeting. As the client manager, you can avoid this scenario – you have tremendous influence to get both parties to begin preparing early. It is almost never too soon to at least float a trial agenda and a shell outline of any written materials.

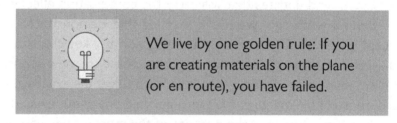

We live by one golden rule: If you are creating materials on the plane (or en route), you have failed.

Avoid Technology Failures

Create all your written or recorded materials and deliver to the client the day before, no exceptions. By doing so, you will accomplish two objectives: ensure the client has notice about any discussion topics and minimize the likelihood of a technology mishap. How many times have you been in a meeting that kicked off ten to fifteen minutes late because of technology? ("What kind of plugin does your computer have? HDMI? VGA?" or "Can you see the screen share?")

In addition, **assume the technology will not work**. For an important meeting, you must have both a belt and suspenders. We encourage our client managers to have an A, B, and (sometimes) C plan. It might look something like this:

For a remote meeting with clients in different cities:

- **Plan A:** Have a screen-share program running (five minutes early) and ask an assistant at the client to ensure it is working on their side before the meeting starts as well.
- **Plan B:** Send the document to the client the day before (as a PDF so it would make it through their firewall limits) and ask an assistant to distribute it to everyone. Walk everyone through the slides using the conference line and announce what page we're on during the presentation.

For an in-person meeting where projecting is preferred:

- **Plan A:** Have the document on your laptop (your hard drive, NOT a share drive requiring VPN and internet access) and the right connector for their projector (call the assistant the day before to ask about what kind of projector they have). Bring an extra mini-projector just in case.
- **Plan B:** Have a reduced-file size version of the documents on a flash drive you can plug directly into your computer if needed.
- **Plan C:** Have enough paper copies for everyone attending.

None of these precautions were observed in the meeting we described at the beginning of this chapter, and it was a train wreck as expected.

 Always assume the technology will not work.

Be Present, Have Presence

This is one of the most important parts of a well-run meeting, as well as excellent career advice: Be present and have presence. Another way of saying this is if you are present in a meeting, you will display presence. Being present means leading the meeting – kicking off with vigor, interacting with the other participants, and avoiding contact/notetaking with your technology (no woobies). We find it to be very common (and distressing) that client managers will introduce subject matter experts in a meeting and subsequently lean back and let everyone talk. Introductions and agenda setting are important but are not a full day's work for a highly compensated client manager. Being present means following the conversation, maintaining eye contact with the speaker, and asking clarifying questions. If you are concerned about looking dumb by asking questions, know that it is certain someone else in the room has the same question. Even if you do look dumb by asking a knowledge-based question, you at least appear intellectually curious and engaged – and you are present. Encourage others to do the same.

The client manager is the coach and the referee for the meeting, all rolled into one. As part of that role, the other participants will need to recognize your role power. By participating actively in the conversation, you will demonstrate your executive presence and be recognized as the coach/referee. In addition, by helping others achieve the same goals, you increase your executive presence. For example, if you have an introverted participant, prepare a slide or two for them to address during the meeting. If not slides, then form a question to specifically call on them to clarify within their scope of expertise. Meeting participants who say nothing do not generate trust, so ensuring everyone has at least a minor contribution will put your client at ease and give them more confidence in the team as a whole.

One minor tip to enhance your client manager presence is to use the name of each participant at least once during the meeting. When making introductions at the beginning, most people will mumble their name and title very quickly. Take the time to clarify names and roles – you will be rewarded with the perception of presence by the participants.

In addition, as the meeting coach, do not assume that the senior leader in the room will lead the meeting. They may on their own, but assume you are the leader until it is obvious otherwise. In a meeting that involves senior leadership from your organization or your client, it is not uncommon for the client manager to kick things off and quickly take a backseat as senior leadership leads the discussion. This is perfectly fine of course, but until it happens, assume you are the leader.

A final word on this important subject – often, early-career folks are given the feedback that they need to improve their "executive presence." As feedback, it seems vague and sinister. Do not worry about "executive presence." Rather, focus on being **present** – and that will be enough. We often say to our teams, "It's not that I pay attention in meetings because I'm a Vice President; I am a Vice President because I pay attention in meetings."

A business card is another nice touch for maintaining an executive presence. Most companies will supply these as part of your onboarding process. However, not every company does. Business cards are old fashioned, and it is entirely possible you will do business with other companies that couldn't care less. Nevertheless, having business cards and presenting them as part of your first meeting with a client conveys a professional presence. Given the fact that electronic touch points continue to evolve, we predict that eventually business cards may be entirely out of fashion. That day is not here yet, so in the meantime, be ready with business cards to demonstrate your commitment to a professional presence.

We occasionally add a third idea to this: Be present, have presence, and **bring presents**. A small gift at the beginning of a meeting can lighten the mood and place everyone in a positive frame of mind. Often the gift does not have to be much more than a company logo-branded tchotchke. Most people are delighted with a small gift, particularly if they were not expecting it. This idea is highly situational depending on your audience (a well-heeled owner or senior executive may not be an appropriate recipient). It's a nice touch, but not required, and only to be used if impactful with the right type of audience.

Video Conferencing

All these concepts hold true, even when video conferencing. In fact, avoiding technology failures and increasing your presence are even more important when meeting virtually. But even if the means are different, the purpose of the meeting is the same: to facilitate a face-to-face interaction.

Test the tech ahead and have a Plan B

Technology failures are even more likely in video conference situations. Prepare ahead of time, particularly if using an unfamiliar technology from your client. Download the software a day early, log in, and ensure it works. Be ready with a Plan B, even if your favorite meeting software is usually reliable. Have your documents ready to be delivered with an alternate means and access to an analog communication solution (e.g., a conference bridge) – this can be a lifesaver when video/screenshare technology goes poorly.

Act like you're in the same room

Being present in this context means engaging in the video call just as you would with a person in the room. No woobies, no typing, no multitasking, and minimize "video bombs." Realistically, your child or dog may make an accidental appearance in a video conference, but try to minimize the likelihood of this. Also, if possible, hide any "self view" on your video screen to minimize your focus on yourself and maximize focus on your client.

The internet is full of advice about how to appear your best on video: clothing, personal appearance, lighting, camera at eye level, stare straight into the camera, etc. We agree some of these ideas are helpful, but we would recommend rather than achieving visual perfection, the above two rules should come first. For the professional client manager, connecting on time and in a professional manner is far more important than using a particular piece of technology. Similarly, less-than-perfect grooming or lighting will quickly be forgotten, but lack of engagement will not. Other considerations, while helpful, are not nearly as important.

After the Meeting

You successfully completed all the meeting steps – now what? **As a best practice, always recap the meeting.** All successful professional sports teams watch recorded coverage the day after the game – so why shouldn't all professional business people review their performance? They should. However, there is a time and place, and the elevator on the way to the parking deck is not it. It seems obvious, but we have horror stories of conversations during elevator rides (with strangers present) that made their way back to the client. Be sure you are firmly off premises before engaging in any conversation about the client or the meeting. We recommend setting a firm rule with your working team that the client or meeting is not discussed until the door is closed as your vehicle drives away. If you have a driver, then wait a while longer – the Uber/cab driver could be a friend of your client!

With that said, the client manager is responsible for getting everyone's feedback and providing the necessary meeting recap. The debrief should include all things positive and negative. **Do not sugarcoat!** Everyone needs to know the temperature of the client, how your company is performing, and what kind of competitive threats might be lurking in the shadows. You should also be very clear on follow-ups/deliverables, who owns them, and the time frame for each. Finally, there should be an internal recap as well as an external recap/meeting minutes that are shared with the client. The external recap is important as it provides clarity to all involved in the meeting that you have agreement on each topic and next steps.

If your organization supports a CRM tool for your clients, enter your debrief materials here as well. This may be tedious but will pay dividends for you later. If you are promoted or for some reason receive a new set of clients, wouldn't you want to be able to see all of the previous context for that client?

To further boost your post-meeting debrief professionalism, also **consider an After-Action Review**. This technique (popularized by the US Army) is a post-event debrief with a focus on what happened during the meeting, why it happened, and how it can be done better in the future. This may require a high level of trust within your team, and some executive presence on your part! However, if you can create a high-trust atmosphere where your meeting team is willing to openly discuss areas where they can improve, this is a very effective meeting debrief technique.

Tactics

1
Prepare something for every client meeting, even when they ask you not to prepare.

2
Send the agenda a day or two ahead of sending any prepared materials to establish a consensus and discover any items the client may want to add. Once the agenda is finalized, share all meeting details in an electronic calendar invite for all parties – this acts as one reference point for all aspects of the meeting, including the agenda, logistics, materials, and conference/screen share details.

3
Avoid technology failures. Check if the room has Wi-Fi, what connectors you'll need, etc. Have back-up plans and materials in case something goes wrong.

4
NO WOOBIES. Keep your technology in your bag. If your laptop will be used for presenting, turn off notifcations and pop-ups.

5
Be present, and interact with participants. Act as a coach, referee, and expert. Control your facial expressions and body language so that even a "dumb" question is handled with kindness and authority.

6
Provide a meeting recap including all positives and negatives, as well as follow-ups/deliverables and who owns them. There should be an internal and external version.

Chapter 10:
The Tricky Art of Client
Entertainment

Fred once went out with a client in what ended up being a very late night. Knowing that the next day was going to be long, he employed a few strategies to minimize the damage:

1. He switched from alcoholic to non-alcoholic beverages on the sly.
2. Knowing it might be a late night (and yes, he knew this client well), Fred made sure everything was ready for the morning (e.g., ironing, shoe shine, alarm).
3. Fred beat the client downstairs for coffee and breakfast the following morning.

Yes, the client was late the next morning (and unwell) so it was up to Fred to lead, and thankfully he was prepared to do so. The client can get away with being late or ill-prepared, but you do not have that option. In this case, by planning ahead, Fred not only managed the client entertainment but also made a massive bank account deposit in the process.

The Rules

Often, the most troubling or least-understood part of managing travel and a client meeting is what happens after the meeting. Navigating the business dinner or cocktail hour can be strenuous – it is a set of norms most people learn over time, without any guidance from their company. It is also highly likely your company has unwritten rules – the least helpful kind. In lieu of more clear guidance, we've found these principles to be generally right.

The importance of planning this portion of the meeting as part of the formal agenda cannot be overestimated. Notionally, the meeting itself is the right time to exchange information and learn what each party is thinking. In practice, we find the most useful strategic information is shared during dinner or at cocktail hour.

 When practical, always schedule social time away from the office with clients and use the time to forge relationships.

Most people are somewhat guarded and on their best behavior while at work or in front of a large audience. However, after a few drinks, your clients are far more likely to corner you and tell you what they really think of your product or service. Use this to your advantage to not only gain intelligence, but also to deepen the relationship.

Client entertainment can take many forms, and we encourage you to be creative and break out of the norm. We've sponsored many client entertainment events over the years – some more mainstream, like a round of golf, and some more unusual, like visiting a shooting range. Be creative, but be aware that the goal of the event is to build a relationship with the client. Anything too extreme may make your client uncomfortable, which is the opposite of your intent.

Fortunately, most client entertainment events will likely be lunch, cocktails, or dinner. We all know rules are made to be broken, and there is no substitute for your own judgment, but we've found these guidelines help make the process of building relationships and trust smoother and more impactful. If you are new to client management or with a new organization, use the following guidelines as industry standard until the unwritten rules become more clear.

Be the host

This is a continuation of your role at the meeting. The host is the person who makes everyone comfortable and interacts good-naturedly. A good way to reinforce this is by how you set the cadence and control the flow of the event. One key thing is to start it off right by making the first toast. Fun!

Let the client invite whomever they want

Getting caught up in who should and shouldn't be invited is not only petty, but it's also an embarrassing conversation that could alienate someone you need in the future. In fact, the client may bring someone worth knowing as you deepen your relationships in their organization and fill in the relationship map.

When would a client ever bring uninvited guests to a business dinner? Fred has experienced this several times. Once, he arranged a client dinner comprised of a pretty large group. The primary executive stated that he could not make the dinner and sent them off with the typical "I am sure you will have a great time without me." The group proceeded to a top-tier steakhouse and ordered cocktails while they waited for their table. To their surprise, the executive walked in — they were delighted! However, instead of joining them for a drink and a meal, this highly paid executive proceeded to order five to-go meals, put it on their tab, and walked out. While there is no doubt that this was a classless act, there was nothing to be done. Even his co-workers were embarrassed and apologized later. Of course, Fred and his team did not make an issue of it — the client relationship is worth far more than the meals!

Level match participants

Level-matching participants is even more important in a social setting. Otherwise, your CEO is talking to the same intern from the meeting but now filled with beer. If the group is a mix of levels, try to navigate seating people next to each other.

When ordering food or beverage, take charge and keep it simple

If dining, take ownership of ordering wine and appetizers for the table. In some cases, you may ask the client to choose wine; regardless, take ownership to avoid any awkwardness.

When ordering your meal, avoid the appearance of someone who is more focused on themselves than the client. As in: "Can I have the salad, but cut the sunflower seeds in half..." We are not offering dietary advice, but rather suggesting that if you have concerns, order something simple. If you have special needs, consider ordering ahead. The client can be as complex as they want, but there's no need to replicate this behavior.

Be kind to the staff

We know this is not you, but some people feel mistreating the host or server is an opportunity to demonstrate toughness and control. Being rude to the waiter or anyone else will reduce trust from your client (and also makes you look like an abusive jerk) – do not do it. Of course, it is okay to speak up for your client if their food is not to their liking – in a respectful fashion. If the client is rude to the waiter, do not intervene. You may want to approach the waiter later and apologize on their behalf; however, as long as you tip well, they will likely be fine.

Tip as you would if it were your money, with a bias toward finishing on a high note. As a rule, in the United States 20% is respectful and appreciated. Even if the service was not deserving of the full 20%, we generally recommend sticking with this guidance – the goal is to end the client entertainment successfully and smoothly. This is not the time to provide feedback to the service staff. Your mission is your client, not fixing another business.

Always, always get the check (or event expenses)

If the client insists on paying, you should make one objection and then let it go. Trust us, this will seldom be an issue! If you are concerned about your ability to expense the dinner or event, get it anyway. The damage you could potentially do to the relationship is far worse than any punishment you will receive for going "too far" with expenses.

Can I Entertain the Client Even If We Are Remote?

Of course! All of this guidance is equally applicable when entertaining clients remotely. We know a client management executive who encourages her team to make "deposit calls" with their clients. No agenda, just client entertainment performed remotely. This can be as simple as a quick check in, but it is even more enhanced with some expense and logistics management.

Order lunch for your client with an online delivery app and enjoy a virtual video lunch. If your expense budget allows it, ship a bottle of wine to your oenophile client and enjoy a virtual wine tasting. Better yet, sign yourself and your client up for an online wine of the month club and schedule a recurring meeting to review the month's wine together. Cover your client's green fees at their favorite course and have them send a smartphone video of them enjoying it. You are only limited by your creativity.

A Word About Expense Management

Many newer client managers will be concerned with some of this advice. You may have concerns that your company is tight with expense management and overspending on client entertainment will "get you in trouble." This is a valid concern, but we've found that most business managers respect that you are "in the field" with a client and making the best decisions you can with your firm's limited resources.

Treat the company's money as your own and you should be fine. If you know you are going to run up a large dinner tab, get clearance in advance from whomever you need to (finance team, your boss, etc.) to minimize later concerns. If you still have concerns, pick a venue more in line with your budget rather than violate these rules.

What If the Fun Never Ends?

Consider what you will do if your client over-indulges or wants to be entertained late. Some clients want to keep going long after the evening's official events have concluded. While this is the exception, it does happen. And you will undoubtedly have a client who overdoes it at least once in your career. Obviously, having a deeper relationship with your client will allow you to predict whether this is likely and plan accordingly. If you have an important client meeting the following day, you may want to give thought to who might be the "sacrifice player" (someone to manage the client late into the evening while you make sure to get adequate rest).

We once worked with a technology executive with an absolutely legendary level of stamina. He would volunteer to be the "late night" client manager and still show up early and chipper the next day for the meeting. We are still not sure how he was able to do this. Most human beings are not that capable, but we loved him for it.

If you do not have someone like this handy, you can consider a graceful way to exit, such as leaving your tab open or asking a responsible party to make sure everyone gets home safely. Regardless, a little planning in this area can pay dividends, as shown in Fred's story at the beginning of this chapter.

The Dangers of Drinks

Although your clients may be bolder and more outspoken after a few drinks, make this a one-way street – there is never any reason for you to share inside information. It may feel good to have a shoulder to cry on about your work difficulties, your insensitive boss, etc., but never indulge yourself in this manner. In addition to the obvious reason that it is unprofessional, it will also subtly tell your client that you cannot hold their proprietary information in confidence. This rule extends in the other direction as well: If your client shares inside information about how their company stinks, their terrible boss, etc., do not consider that an invitation to pile on. A sympathetic ear is your only responsibility, and any more than that risks reducing overall trust in the relationship.

Why do any of these things happen? One word: alcohol. Beware the dangers of alcohol, and **limit yourself to one or at most two drinks during any business function**. As the client manager, in order to maintain control of the social event, it is your job to make sure neither you nor anyone else on your team over-imbibes. This is easier said than done, particularly if you are with a close, long-time client that likes to "have fun."

You can always control yourself, but what if one of your executives who outranks you considerably decides this would be a great time for a bender? Or worse yet, a senior executive from the client? He or she has no kids to go home to and put in bed; the company is paying for it, so why not? This happens more often than you might think – we've poured several executives (who should know better) into their hotel room after a lengthy cocktail hour. In this scenario,

stay close to the executive. Be an active listener, and be on the lookout for anything inappropriate. Keep an eye on the bartender to ensure your wayward executive is not ordering doubles. When you get the chance, shut it down in the quietest fashion possible. Do not confront them; instead, make an excuse to get "back to the hotel for a nightcap."

Harassment and Sticky Situations

Client entertainment is an excellent way to build relationships – until it goes terribly wrong. All of our above advice is predicated on the idea that the work environment is relatively safe… but what if it is not? What if you as a client manager take your client to dinner, follow all the rules, and later it becomes obvious that the client's interest is not professional? What if the senior client leader (notionally a level or two above you) wants to spend time together after dinner (to your initial delight), but their version of "relationship building" is a clear quid pro quo? What if you have to pour a drunk executive into their room? What do you do when the two of you are different genders? Is that an acceptable situation?

These are complex issues. Harassment can occur in any setting in the workplace, between all genders. However, we know that for client managers, it typically happens in a social framework rather than in the office. Often, in-office client meetings are well attended, and all attendees are on their best behavior. This can change rapidly once everyone is away from the office, and clients can take advantage of their vendor relationship to prey upon the client manager. The fact that the harassment occurs across company lines makes the situation twice as complex. We would argue this form of harassment is much worse than "routine" workplace harassment because the harasser is likely taking advantage of the client manager's desire to please and the economic nature of the relationship.

Compounding the issue is the reality that many workplaces are already not receptive to accusations of harassment. Many managers and HR personnel are notorious for minimizing the legitimate concerns of employees. Now consider what happens when the complaint is not about an internal team member, but rather a third party – one that the company depends upon for revenue. Companies that already minimize these issues will likely be even more reticent to solve a harassment issue with a client.

We certainly hope you are in a workplace that is supportive of consideration of these issues and will investigate thoroughly. Regardless of that reality, we would suggest the following steps to proactively deal with the issue.

Always meet tag team

If you suspect a client may want more than a professional relationship, always meet tag team. A colleague from your company (or theirs), a friend – anyone will do. Even if your client asks specifically to meet alone for dinner, drinks, etc., bring someone with you – even if you have to offer a flimsy excuse to do so. Do not let any potential awkwardness prevent you from caring for your safety as the primary concern. Making your client comfortable is very low on the list of priorities when it comes to avoiding harassment.

Work out an excuse to leave ahead of time

Thinking about this ahead of time will make the requirement more credible ("Sorry, I have to get up early for a flight."). Your tag-team partner can also help in this regard with their own reason for leaving and why you need to leave with them. Your wing-person does not have to wear a sandwich board proclaiming their role. They should know in advance that they have a two-drink maximum and are 100% "working."

If you cannot bring a colleague, always conduct business in an open setting

If in a bar, meet in the main bar area, not a dimly lit booth. If at a restaurant, request a table in the middle of the dining room. Only meet in a hotel lobby, never in a client's hotel room (do not even drop off someone at their room if there is even a possibility of harassment). Let someone else handle that job.

For transportation, use ride sharing

Do not offer or accept an offer to be alone with a potential harasser in a vehicle. Ridesharing gives you a witness in the car as well as a trackable record of where you have been and the time(s) you were there. Again, this may create awkwardness ("Hey, my car is right here!"), but it's well worth it in the end. Perhaps it is a relationship debit with the client, but remember some debits are inevitable and even necessary.

Document the incident

Most importantly, document the incident thoroughly, even when you manage to successfully diffuse the harassment. We cannot stress this enough. Even if you manage to successfully disengage from the potential harasser, write down everything that happened in fine detail. Document the place of the harassment, time, circumstances, other attendees, and any other relevant details. Do not let the fact that you dissuaded your harasser lead you to believe that "everything is fine." In fact, these situations often have a way of becoming worse over time. Your harasser will very likely interpret your reticence as "playing hard to get" and will only redouble their efforts the next time you interact. When the issue comes to a head, whoever is involved (your manager, HR, your lawyer) will view you with greater credibility if you have documentation. You must perform this critical step even if you do not immediately report it to your management or HR. It is very tempting to brush off early-stage harassment as flirting or dismiss it with, "Well, everyone had too much to drink." Assume it is not a one-time incident. If the harassment gets worse, a well-documented timeline of escalation will go a long way in ensuring your company does the right thing.

Should you report the issue to HR and your management?

The answer is almost always yes. In the US, it is illegal for a workplace to retaliate against you for reporting harassment. If you do not report the harassment, you may lose some of your rights in any future litigation. Any moderately worthwhile management team will appreciate the gravity of the issue and, at the very least, reassign the client manager. Most HR departments are sensitive to these complaints and will at least make sure you are not placed in a situation where the harassment will continue.

We know there are workplaces where this is not the case – where dismissal of concerns and retaliation are the norm. Client-related harassment can increase that probability. In those cases, we recommend retaining an employment lawyer. Because you documented the harassment in excruciating detail, you are in a much better position to create a better outcome.

Tactics

1 Remember that you're the host at any client event or meal. Take charge of ordering appetizers and wine for the table, and be prepared to give the first toast.

2 The first toast does not need to be a speech. You can keep it simple by expressing thanks for the great meeting.

3 Know your company rules about expense management, but when in doubt, don't create discomfort for the client.

4 Your client is watching how you interact with the staff – be kind and tip within expected norms.

5 When it comes to issues like over-indulgence and sexual harassment, "the client is never wrong" thinking **does not apply**.

Chapter 11:
Communicate

Effective, accurate, and efficient communication is the key to success regardless of the nature of your job. Whether your audience is internal, external, executive level, or entry level, it doesn't matter – communication is a linchpin skill.

Early in his career, Fred was tasked with organizing and managing the company's first ever Six Sigma project. The success of this project would be defined by solid project management, a strong command of the Six Sigma discipline, and buy-in from all the affected parties. One Friday afternoon, he crafted a weekly update email highlighting successes and struggles for the entire team as well as sponsoring executives. One struggle was the ability to get a certain level of detailed data, not for lack of effort. However, in the Friday afternoon rush to complete the task, Fred made this a simple bullet point: "Still struggling to get XX data points."

Without the proper clarification as to why this was a problem, the assumption – and the blame – was quickly placed on the person who owned this task, Steve. The "still" in "still struggling" probably did not help. Naturally, Steve wanted to clarify/defend himself, which he did and then some. With everyone on copy, Steve clarified the nature of the "struggle" and went on to share his thoughts (all negative) regarding the leadership of the project. This response hit Fred's inbox over the weekend and hung over him like a dark cloud.

On Monday morning, Fred's SVP summoned him to her office and asked what this was about. Once he clarified, Fred's boss asked how he would respond. Fred felt attacked and wanted to "reply all" to set the record straight, but knowing that this would result in more emails and immaturity, he elected to call Steve. They talked through the miscommunication and collaborated on an email that set the record straight.

All of this extra work was avoidable and only necessary because both parties were dealing in a low-context medium. It is unlikely that anyone remembers Fred's status update (or anything about this project for that matter) – but they will remember Fred's professionalism (and Steve's lack thereof).

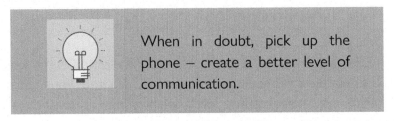

When in doubt, pick up the phone – create a better level of communication.

When in Doubt, Communicate

We are often asked by newer client managers, "Should I communicate this to the client?" The answer is always simple: **If the thought even occurs to you to communicate something, then communicate it.** With that said, exactly what you communicate, how you communicate, and the medium and tone of communication should all be considered quite carefully.

With this chapter, we cover some general ideas for client manager communications, with a specific focus on written communications – the riskiest type.

Email as Business Communication

Email was a revolution in business communication. It is efficient, timely, and accessible. It is also the most commonly used type of written business communication. With that said, it is also fraught with risk regarding interpretation, intention, and tone. No one receives any formal education on how to write an effective email. Odd, considering many client managers will tell you they spend a significant portion of their day communicating through email! Email provides the least amount of context (e.g., tone, body language, etc.) and is therefore the most subject to misinterpretation and subsequent relationship debits. The combination of least discussed, most used, and most subject to misinterpretation makes email (as well as business writing in general) worthy of special attention.

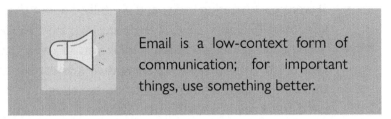

Email is a low-context form of communication; for important things, use something better.

There are multiple methods of written communication available today that replace email, such as group chat programs or instant messaging. Most of these have the same challenges as email, but email is still the most popular means of communication between businesses, so for now we'll stick with email as the broad term for all of these types of communication.

The internet is full of listicles on "How to send more effective email," with banal suggestions like "always use the subject line" or "don't use abbreviations." Most of this advice is well intentioned but hard to remember in the day-to-day. In addition, great communication builds relationships naturally. We'll skip the typical advice here and instead focus on five top-level processes to always ensure high-quality, relationship-building communications.

Bottom line up front: Always start with the conclusion

It can be a question, required action, or an answer. Regardless, it is the point of the email and the associated action. If the email is a statement, then the action may just be informational – so state that up front. If it is a question, include the fact that you need a reply. If there is a required action, state what you need the recipient to do. Business email is not meant for storytelling. Save your storytelling for a meeting or presentation. Most executives and other buyers of your service are too busy to receive all the backstories first. To that end, do not think of yourself as an email writer; think of yourself as an email **re-writer**, with your entire goal to begin with the end in mind and be more succinct. Most emails are written as a stream of consciousness from the writer and immediately sent, and it shows. Which email would you rather receive?

- "I went to a meeting today and we talked about the upcoming IT audits. One of the things we talked about was the client's infosec audit. I think you all know that they are thinking about upgrading their standards, and they are sending in a big team to do the audit. What we didn't know is that the new standards will require us to change how we manage our VPN routing. So, the IT VP spent some time telling us that we might as well start soon reconfiguring the router. We brainstormed and kicked around some ideas, and we agreed that we'll need to upgrade to a new software vendor and have it installed by June."
- "We will upgrade our VPN routing software to a new vendor and complete installation by June.
  - The client's upcoming infosec audit requires new, upgraded standards.
  - They are sending a large team to ensure the standard.
  - We will begin immediately."

When communicating in a written form, write what is inside of you – it will probably look more like the first example – then come back and **rewrite it** to look more like the second. Your clients (and in particular executives) will thank you for your brevity. You can still include the small touches to indicate you value the relationship (thanking the client for the last meeting, making a request pleasantly), but structure it with concision in mind.[1]

Be positive – very positive

Assume your recipient will read your email 30% more negatively than what you intended. Right or wrong, most written communication in business tends to be interpreted negatively. It utterly lacks the context about the sender's state of mind.

---

[1] Crisp, well-written communications are well worth a deeper dive. Fortunately, there are plenty of materials to make you a better communicator – we've included several excellent reference books in the **Resources**.

Read this sentence and ask yourself whether the tone is appropriate:

"We need to take ownership of this problem."

A common enough sentiment in business. What is the context? Does the "we" include the writer, or is it a passive-aggressive attack on the ownership level of the recipient? Or is the writer viewing this positively and rallying everyone to the cause? If that is the case, perhaps we could say, "We need to take ownership of this problem!!" Or did that make it worse because it seems like yelling?

Remember: Your recipient is likely at work and under pressure to perform. They just left a meeting where the boss reviewed revenue targets or a missed deadline. Upon receipt of your email, now they are under even more stress because you "obviously" meant something negative.

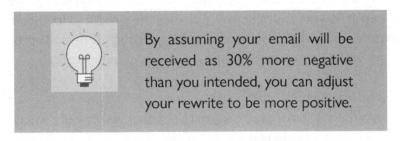

By assuming your email will be received as 30% more negative than you intended, you can adjust your rewrite to be more positive.

How does the following look as an alternative?

"We need to take ownership of this problem, starting with my team. We will have the revised plans to you by Monday! We'll solve this together."

Perhaps a bit less brief, but it reduces the risk of the email being misinterpreted and creating an accidental relationship debit.

In addition, do not include negativity towards any particular individual (or team), whether internal to your organization or external. Consider these examples when taking responsibility for an issue:

- "The customer service team did not deliver this for you. We will work to make it better."
- "We did not deliver this for you. We will work to make it better."

With this simple change, the client manager has taken ownership of any wrongdoing and communicated a sense of "we" — not you, us, or them.

Assume the email will be forwarded

A final reason for a positive tone: Always assume the email will be forwarded. That recipient (perhaps an individual only tangentially aware of your relationship) will have even less context around your issue. Never assume any level of confidentiality with any email that you write, particularly if the email has negative content. The legalese contained in many corporate emails that prohibits forwarding does not protect you from an inadvertent relationship debit! To that end, maintain an overly positive tone in email to prevent those consequences. Save the debits for when you really need them, not for something as trivial as email.

None of this should imply that your communication should be covered in flowers and rainbows. You must be direct and forthcoming about negative issues. However, thinking through tone and verbiage will go a long way toward ensuring effective communication.

Don't forward emails

As the client manager, it is also critical that you do not compound a problem by forwarding the email, unless it is to generate productive work. In our time leading account teams, we have received dozens of emails from client managers that were forwarded from a client with commentary such as "Can you believe these guys?" There are two downsides to this behavior. First, it is not productive — your team cannot help you win with the client if your communication is venting. It is much better to acknowledge in an unemotional way the nature of the challenge and focus most of your energy on remediation. Secondly, it sets you up for failure later — because your team will be much more likely to discount a client's request in the future. The next time you need a teammate to help you execute with the client, they will instead bring up that your client is "unreasonable," and your ability to execute for your client will be impaired. It is your role to keep your team focused on resolution, not further exacerbate the situation by forwarding such an email with a "What the heck?" Always focus on resolution.

Leverage technology to correct grammatical and usage errors

You are already familiar with basic word processing tools such as spell check and sentence fragment check. However, most emails contain poor writing, not just spelling or syntax errors. Every day, we see comma misplacement, passive voice, clichés, and other writing errors. However, as a practical matter, your ability to remember all the style points of good writing is limited – you are a busy client manager trying to grow a business. If you do read Strunk and White[2] we absolutely applaud you, but this is probably not a reasonable expectation for most client managers.

Good news: Technology to analyze and error-correct writing has improved considerably in the past ten years. Even very standardized tools such as those bundled with Microsoft Word now have the ability to check for an incredible variety of syntax and style errors beyond the usual spell check (most of these tools are not default settings and require activation). Popular online programs can be downloaded as plug-ins to many email programs. Many will also include the Fleisch readability index, which measures the readability of your email. The cost is minimal for most (and can usually be expensed) – invest in one today, and you will be glad you did.

As a note of caution, your client can be as informal as they want, but that does not mean that you should follow suit. Informality can be a powerful tool that strengthens the relationship on a personal level – but pick your moments wisely.

We once had a client who used ellipses at an abusive level... we think maybe he thought it gave his writing an aura of mystery... or maybe not... It sure made for weird reading. He was a great businessperson, and it was his style. We also worked with a very senior, experienced salesperson who abbreviated every word he possibly could. If you needed add'l info from his comms it was s'times hard to understand.

---

[2] We list some popular technology products and guides for writing style in the **Resources**.

Written communication is for the reader, not the writer.

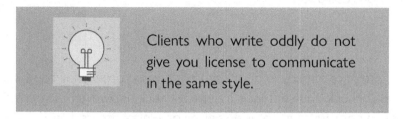

Clients who write oddly do not give you license to communicate in the same style.

Again, assume anything you send to a client will get forwarded to senior leaders. Keep it brief, positive, and well written (with the help of technology).

Email as Danger

Everyone has received an email and upon first glance inferred a tone of anger or animosity. If you recall our earlier discussions about written communications, you might reconsider whether the sender really did have negative intent. For any overly abrupt email you receive, be assured that there are other forces at play. Your client is under pressure beyond their control.

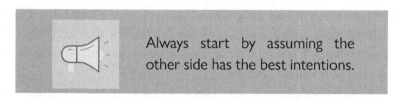

Always start by assuming the other side has the best intentions.

Regardless, even if the sender had the intent to harm, we would caution against any kind of immediate reply. Particularly when the email is critical of you or your product directly, an instinctive fight-or-flight response is easily triggered, and the easiest way to deal with the issue is a return email to continue the fight. But don't do it; take the high road! The best course is to get a cup of coffee and give that email some time to marinate. Realize that the intent may not be the same as your interpretation. What did the sender of the email actually intend to convey?

For any communication with strong emotional content, wait at least overnight before replying

One technique we've often used is to write the email, save it, and rewrite it the next day. Documenting your initial response can be cathartic. But the next day's clear head will probably bring a different, better frame of mind. Your ability to deal with the issue on an emotional level will be vastly improved by a good night's rest. One amendment to this technique is to show your work to another client manager. They will probably approach the issue from a much more rational place as well and provide needed perspective.

When to Go Face-to-Face (or Ear-to-Ear)

In any of the preceding scenarios, **immediately suggest an in-person meeting, screen share, or phone conversation – anything to increase the level of context**. Remember, for important communications, avoid email and use something better. A higher-level form of conversation will immediately improve context and allow for clearer, less emotional communication. Many people are "brave" in email but less so in a direct conversation.

Think through what types of communication will always require a high-context medium. For example, in many industries, any kind of security, privacy, or safety issue may require direct, high-context communication rather than a routine email. In a technology context, a severity one incident report (like an outage) may require immediate attention and continuous client updates – best done over the phone. In any of these serious events, you are the face of the organization. Take ownership and inform your client that you own the resolution. Provide the client with the reassurance that the issue has your undivided attention. Then move promptly to rally the internal team and make sure the issue is addressed appropriately.

Take some time now to define for yourself what types of issues will require immediate contact with the client. This may seem silly (you may think to yourself, "I'll know it when I see it"), but we've found that many client managers freeze in a crisis, unsure how to handle the situation while waiting for senior management to direct the client contact. Knowing that step one may be high-context communication will speed up your decision-making process.

Upon resolution, a thorough report may be warranted, and email may be the ideal medium for this type of follow-through. We like the idea of sharing an "incident report" including an executive summary, issue, timeline, short-term corrective action, and long-term corrective action. Your format may vary. Nevertheless, this is an excellent way to take ownership and apologize for the issue with some of the techniques we reviewed in Chapter 3.

One type of communication is always a candidate for a high-context conversation: relationship withdrawals. When the organization asks us to communicate bad news to the client, the temptation is to go low-context ("I'll just email!"), which is almost always the wrong choice. Painful as it is, as a client manager you are paid to communicate effectively, and withdrawals are worth a high-context medium.

When making a withdrawal, also consider timing. Do you really need to give your client bad news at 4:00pm on a Friday afternoon on a holiday weekend? Sometimes the answer is yes (privacy, security, safety), but most of the time it can wait. You should always ask, "Will having this information today vs. at a later date impact the situation in any way?"

We also have one other golden rule for moving away from email: If an email has more than three "reply-alls," call a meeting. Nothing is more irritating than being the recipient of dozens of emails or group chats because the communication medium is wrong. Email is an excellent channel for low-emotion, high-volume communication. It is completely ill-suited for negotiations between parties, which usually manifests itself as an email debate. Be the client manager who cuts off that behavior and moves the discussion to where it belongs – as a discussion.

Consider timing in a 24/7 world

In a previous life, Fred worked for a CFO who was "on" 24/7. The CFO would send emails at any time on any day. In an attempt to please his boss, acclimate to a new culture, and create an overall good impression, Fred would respond as quickly as possible. This usually created a disruption to Fred's downtime and/or family time. After about three months, Fred went to the CFO in an effort to establish expectations. To Fred's relief, the CFO stated that he did not expect immediate responses late at night or on the weekends. The CFO stated, "If I need an immediate response, you will know it." That was one of the most valuable conversations of Fred's career. It was also one of the most valuable lessons. As Fred's career grew, from a leadership perspective he vowed to never put any of his team members in that situation. When catching up in the evening or on the weekend, Fred would keep all emails in his draft folder and send them out in the morning.

The same discipline and logic hold true externally. Is this an email or message that your client needs right now? It also behooves client managers to have similar conversations with their client: "Mr. Client, I see that you are often on email from 10:30 to 11:30pm. I am typically with my family at such time. I assume you are cleaning your inbox, but I wanted to check in with you to make sure our expectations are aligned." Regardless of the client's response, you just made a deposit.

Know Your Audience

We often get the advice as email writers (or as presenters) to "know your audience" — but what does that really mean? Does it mean if the audience is executive, I should keep it brief? Or if a more operational audience, include all of the details?

It is tempting to think of knowing your audience as being a judgment about how busy the person is — and therefore their ability to consume information. We believe it is much more important to attempt to tailor your message based on a reasonable guess about how the recipient consumes information. This might be difficult unless you place some sort of frame around how other people think. It is easy to generalize around surface attributes (e.g., "This person is smart," or "This person prefers a verbal update."). To get to the next level of understanding, **we recommend you (and your company if possible) adopt a framework for understanding the mindset of others**. For your clients, it generally will not be possible to actually survey them to understand their ways of processing information. If you have a framework that you commonly use, you can at least make a reasonable guess about your client counterpart. That educated guess is usually enough information to tailor your emails, presentations, or verbal communications to communicate effectively. All of these frameworks are non-judgmental, meaning that they are about preferences and thinking; there are no "good" or "bad" types here. Thus, this is a way to think about clients without making judgments like good or bad, smart or dumb, effective or ineffective.

Many of these frameworks have free or low-cost online assessments for you to take yourself. We highly recommend doing so because not only will you gain more insight into your own preferences, but you'll develop insight into your client's as well. Here are a few popular frameworks, each of which has merit:

- **DiSC** – Focused on interpreting behavioral preferences around four quadrants: Dominance, Influence, Steadiness, Conscientiousness. We like this profile template because it is easy to understand and remember. For a busy client manager, this framework is the easiest to apply to other people in communications. For example, a high D will want simple facts whereas a high S may want more details. However, it is not as detailed or sophisticated as other frameworks.
- **Myers-Briggs (MBTI)** – Probably the best-known assessment. Frames the test-taker's mode of thinking and information-processing dominance in addition to personality. More complex with four variables, each having two dimensions. Some attributes (like Intuitive vs. Sensing thinking) are harder to guess in others.
- **Herrmann Brain Dominance Instrument (HBDI)** – Analysis of an individual's type of thinking: Analytical, Sequential, Interpersonal, or Imaginative. Relatively easy to understand and very good for thinking through how someone absorbs information.
- **StrengthsFinder** – Relatively new measurement from Gallup, more focused on understanding a person's natural talents. Based on deep Gallup research on

what makes for successful managers and employees. Somewhat complex (and therefore may not be good for guessing communication styles), but very insightful.

Thinking style frameworks can also help you understand how others communicate to you. You do not have to know someone's exact Myers-Briggs or DiSC makeup; you can often gather this via their communications. Fred remembers working with an individual who was very curt in his emails. When they began working together, Fred was often taken aback by the terse nature of these written communications. He wondered if somehow he was miscommunicating with or misinterpreting his colleague. After some time working together, Fred gained an understanding and appreciation for his style. The colleague ran all of Europe for their client, was incredibly busy, and simply didn't have time for pleasantries. He was trying to get the job done. Thinking through his profile, he was probably a high D (driver) for DiSC or high S (sequential) for HBDI. If ever Fred received an email that felt overtly abrasive, he would respond by phone. The phone interactions were always pleasant and quickly dispelled any perceived tension. They had a very productive relationship because Fred knew his audience (and it didn't hurt that he always assumed positive intent).

Several of these types of behavioral inventories have critics. Many are not based on research and may leave out critical elements of understanding human thinking. We are not social psychologists and would not try to refute any of those arguments. Our point is that you will need a system to classify individuals so you can tailor your communications – which framework you use may be less important than choosing one and using it consistently, even if imperfect. Regardless of whether you invest in one of these tools, at least a few minutes of thought about your recipient's communication style can save hours of work crafting the right message.

Listening vs. Talking

We've mentioned it several times, but it cannot be stated enough: There is no downside to listening, and the upside is enormous. In fact, you may notice that at least three of our Client Management

Philosophies are directly related to listening. It is the most powerful tool in the client manager's toolkit and generally the least utilized.

Unfortunately, for some of us (high E in Myers-Briggs or high D/I in DiSC) it is also unnatural. As client managers we carry so much (product, service, relationship) expertise, we feel we have to share it with the world. Some of us are just bursting with ideas and knowledge that we know our clients will love. Additionally, in an effort to build rapport, we are quick to come up with a similar story to share. The problem with either scenario is that even if we aren't talking, we are no longer listening. We've moved ahead of the conversation by preparing our response, and in doing so we miss out on valuable information.

We know you have read this before or received this feedback – nothing new here. You know that listening to your clients is the right thing to do, and you intend to do it in each and every client meeting. But somehow, it gets away from you, and instead you wind up controlling the conversation.

Rather than convince you of the merits of active listening, we offer a challenge: In your next client meeting, offer no solutions, opinions, or advice. In other words, for one meeting take time off from what you reasonably view as your job and only focus on understanding everything you can about your client (maybe even ask some of the personal questions from Chapter 2 – aha!). Come armed with a list of questions as conversation starters if needed, but take a break from controlling the meeting. This may be a struggle – being in listening mode can often feel like you are not doing anything. Rest assured your client will feel differently.

What will the results be? We guarantee you will come away with a newfound respect for the power of listening. You will realize you have deepened the relationship, built trust, and learned something. We expect you will also find out something new and surprising about your client, relevant enough to document in your client relationship management software. Something that will make you say, "I am really glad I did that, and I'm going to spend more time listening in the future."

Tactics

Quality communications are all about tactics – getting the details right to ensure your message is heard.

1

Answer yes/no questions directly.

We often see new client managers talking around an issue in answer to a direct question, particularly when they feel put on the spot about execution.

For example, a client may ask, "Does your product work with the XYZ industry standard?" The client manager then replies, "Well, what you need to know about the XYZ industry standard is…" and then proceeds to set the context. That can be valuable, and it is important to educate clients. Unfortunately, somewhere in the middle of a long digression about industry standards, the customer never received a direct yes or no answer.

Provide firm responses to direct questions, and your client will thank you for valuing their time. You can always add additional context, such as: "We don't do that today, but we're thinking of adding that feature. One thing to remember is the older industry standards may be rewritten next year…"

2

Thank them for their business.

It's a nice touch that reminds them that you value the relationship and you view them as more than a source of revenue.

We often use this at a major milestone, like renewing a contract or completing a major project. It can be as simple as an email sign-off or as elaborate as a handwritten thank-you card. It is a very small touch, but your client will appreciate your relationship investment.

3 | Make a commitment.

Often, client managers will want to avoid committing their organization to a course of action because they are not sure if their organization can deliver. This can be a valid concern!

Nevertheless, determine something that you can commit to as part of your communication. For example, "We'll look into whether we meet the XYZ standard. I'll get back to you by Tuesday," or "I know we'll find a solution to this problem. It may not be as soon as next week, but I can commit to solving it by next month."

Make some level of commitment to make relationship deposits as well as enable crisp communications.

4 | No jump balls.

We once worked for an individual who would admonish you for "jump balls" – communicating action items but not assigning them to an owner. As a newer client manager, you may not feel confident giving people more senior than you "to-dos" (and we often see senior client managers forgetting this important step).

When assigning follow-up tasks (both internal and external), actually assign them to an individual. Steve owns X. Sally will deliver Y.

Without that direct ownership, everyone will assume that someone else has it. If you are concerned they may reject ownership or that they are not the right owner, the best way to invite that conversation is to make the assignment anyway. The recipient of your action may disagree, but at least you will make progress towards finding an owner.

Wrap Up
& Resources

Wrap Up

We hope you have found this book useful. Just by reading it, you have demonstrated your willingness to learn and grow in the client management role, which already puts you ahead of your peers. Now it's time to get out there and execute! We'll leave you with a few final thoughts.

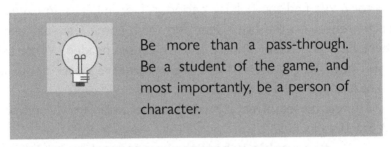

Be more than a pass-through. Be a student of the game, and most importantly, be a person of character.

Be More than a Pass-Through

Be the kind of client manager who adds tremendous value in every interaction with the client and your internal organization. We know some client managers (not the good ones) that are merely "pass-throughs" for their organization. They take requirements from their customers and pass them on to the rest of the organization. After reading this book, we know that will not be you.

When you demonstrate ownership of your clients (the good, the bad, and everything in between), you will differentiate yourself as a client manager who leads by demonstrating excellent character, not just expertise.

Be a Student of the Game

With this book, we've explored only the surface-level knowledge sufficient to be a good client manager. Every topic is worthy of its own specialized study, whether it be building relationships, project management, value selling, or written communications. There is so much left to learn! With experience comes wisdom, but you can begin sooner than you think on that journey.

The resources listed at the end of this book are just the beginning – we encourage you to explore further. Each topic will aid you in your journey toward becoming a more complete businessperson. Many companies claim to make investments in their teams with skill development programs, but few companies actually do this. Independent of your company's policies, resolve to craft an annual development plan for your client management skills.

There are simple ways to make this part of your yearly routine, but the practice will have a profound effect on your long-term career trajectory. We find the holiday period in December is an excellent time to reflect on the prior year and think about the year ahead. Where have you been? Where is your career headed? What skills do you need to get there? Have you received feedback about any weaknesses you need to address?

There is no set format for a development plan, however, several best practices include:

1. **Actionable is better than formal.** A development plan written on notebook paper and taped to your monitor is 100 times better than one formally entered into your company's HR system, never to be seen again.

2. **One major goal is better than many.** We've seen development plans with five books to read, two conferences, job shadowing, and a week-long class. When was that person planning to do their work? Better to set one stretch goal and actually achieve it.

3. **Make it measurable.** Most development plans start with a notion of being "better" but lack specificity:
   - "This year, I will be better at presenting value propositions."
   - Much better: "I will complete a 20-hour online seminar on developing and presenting value propositions by May. I will use what I have learned in three client presentations before the end of the year."

What makes for great development plan content? Again, the goal is yours, but the investment does not necessarily have to be money. For example, if you are nervous about public speaking, Toastmasters[1] is a low-cost resource that can help you grow as a public speaker. Is there a role in your company that you view as your next career step? Ask to shadow the person in that role for three days. Do you want to learn to code? Ask your boss if you can attend a week-long training event.

The resources to invest in yourself are only limited by your creativity. We often meet client managers who tell us their boss or company does not invest in their growth. We say, "Invest in yourself first, and your company will follow."

Final Thought: A Word About Character

Job #1 is to build a relationship, and therefore build trust. You won't be able to do either if you are not a person of integrity and character. We've seen business leaders who lack character succeed for some time but rarely for the long run. Character is destiny, even for a client manager striving to grow clients in a business setting.

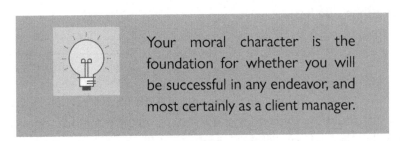

Your moral character is the foundation for whether you will be successful in any endeavor, and most certainly as a client manager.

We know you did not pick up this book to be a better person but rather to understand the techniques you need to be a successful client manager. As it turns out, each of the Principles of Client Management is based on character traits fundamental to business success. We merely translated old-fashioned virtues into modern language more relatable to everyday business.

---

[1] www.toastmasters.org

Philosophy	Character Trait
Seek to understand, then to be understood.	Empathy, Humility
We need each other. Our relationship is not a zero-sum game.	Loyalty, Patience
Concentrate on material issues, not the small stuff...	Wisdom, Forbearance
...but on the other hand, if it's easy, then just do it.	Industry, Diligence
Email is a low-context form of communication. For important things, use something better.	Courage, Sincerity
Always start by assuming the other side has the best intentions.	Respect, Tolerance

You may wonder what happened with Mitch, our client from the introduction who morphed into a dragon before our very eyes. In the end, we listened, addressed his concerns, and created a productive client relationship, making it clear that the dragon was not needed to ensure the success of the relationship. Ultimately, we did not develop a relationship with Mitch just because we executed the techniques in this book, but also because we acted with integrity and character in every interaction. With that relationship came trust and growth.

We challenge you to do the same — infuse your client management skills with your fundamental decency, and you will reap the benefits. We are rooting for you!

Resources

Further Study

Building Relationships

Carnegie, Dale. *How to Win Friends and Influence People*. Simon & Schuster, 2009.

Schwartz, David J. *The Magic of Thinking Big*. Touchstone, 2015.

Client Management Philosophies

Covey, Steven. *The Seven Habits of Highly Effective People*. Mango, 2016.

Communication Logic and Structure

Minto, Barbara. *The Pyramid Principle*. Prentice-Hall, 2010.

Zelazny, Gene. *Say It with Presentations: How to Design and Deliver Successful Business Presentations*. McGraw-Hill, 2006.

Zelazny, Gene. *Say It with Charts: The Executive's Guide to Visual Communication*. McGraw-Hill, 2001.

Emotions in Decision-Making

Dane, Erik, and Jennifer M. George. "The Hidden Role of Emotion in Decision Making." *Rice Business Wisdom*, 30 Jan. 2018, **business.rice.edu/wisdom/peer-reviewed-research/hidden-role-emotion-decision-making**.

Edge, Deckle. *Predictably Irrational*. Harper, 2009.

Gino, Francesca. "Don't Let Emotions Screw Up Your Decisions." *Harvard Business Review*, 6 May 2015, **hbr.org/2015/05/dont-let-emotions-screw-up-your-decisions**.

Grammar

Strunk, William, and E.B White. *Elements of Style*. Pearson, 2019.

Negotiations

Fisher, Roger and William Ury. *Getting to Yes: Negotiating Agreement Without Giving In*. Random House, 1981.

Neale, Margaret and Max Bazerman. *Negotiating Rationally*. Free Press, 1991.

Shell, Richard. *Bargaining for Advantage*. Viking, 1999.

OKRs

Doerr, John. *Measure What Matters: How Google, Bono, and the Gates Foundation Rock the World with OKRs*. Portfolio, 2018.

Storytelling and Value Proposition

Heath, Chip and Dan Heath. *Made to Stick*. Random House, 2007.

Rackham, Neil. *Spin Selling*. McGraw-Hill, 1988.

Tools and Software

Grammar

Ginger Software, **www.gingersoftware.com**

Grammarly, **www.grammarly.com**

MS Word: Enable "Grammar and Refinements" and "Readability Statistics" in **Options – Proofing**.

Project Management

Airtable, **www.airtable.com**

Asana, **www.asana.com**

Monday, **www.monday.com**

Public Speaking

Toastmasters, **www.toastmasters.org**

Example Account Review

Widget Corp Account Review
Client: Woobie Blankets

Relationship Manager: Jimmy Smith
Account Engineer: Brad Beantown

Principal / Relationship

Principal	Relationship
CEO Woobie: Billy Willy	Enthusiastic fan of Widget Corp.
CFO Woobie: Nilly Willy	Concerned with price and Widget delivery issues
Controller Woobie: Sally Willy	Neutral; likes product but not invoicing issues
Buyer Woobie: Wally Willy	Detractor; believes Widget overpriced and did not deliver on new product launches
Marketing Woobie: Jill Willy	Neutral; not engaged

Key Issues and Initiatives

Strategic
- Views our raw materials as very strategic
- Some rumors that Woobie may be capital constrained

Product
- Recently launched new "Supersoft Woobies" with our materials, but no marketing behind it yet
- Would like Widget Corp to invest in new products
- Recently raised prices for their main product, "Medium-Soft Woobies"

Operational
- Very intent to operationalize new manufacturing process
- Recently asked to adjust to 90-days to pay
- Need to adjust Widget package size to fit their warehouse storage

Growth
- Good growth in smaller markets with "Medium-Soft Woobies"
- Need more engagement from Jill Willy, marketing lead, to emphasize value of Widget materials in "Supersoft Woobies"
- Widget needs to co-invest marketing dollars with Woobie

Revenue from Woobie

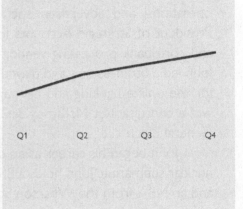

157

About the Authors

John Brown

John Brown has over 25 years of experience as a client manager and operations leader. He is currently Chief Operating Officer at ParkMobile. Previously, John was Vice President of Client Operations at Clutch Technologies. He built the bank client-facing team at Cardlytics, including bank sales, implementations, technical operations, and advertiser operations. Before that he was Vice President of Strategic Accounts for Fiserv, a leading online banking and core bank processing vendor. During his seven years at Fiserv, John led a business unit and played a key role in strategy formulation for the online banking and bill pay businesses. Prior to Fiserv, John was a consultant at McKinsey & Co. and a sales representative with General Electric.

John began his career as an officer in the U.S. Navy onboard a nuclear submarine. John holds a BS in Physics from Tulane University and an MBA from the Wharton School of Business.

Fred Fuller

With over 20 years of corporate experience, Fred Fuller has worked with a number of technology companies in several capacities. Upon graduating from college with a BBS in Decision Sciences, Fred started his corporate career in the world of finance, where he provided financial guidance for business units around the globe. He later moved into a client management role, where he took responsibility for the entire Financial Institution Account Management team at Cardlytics, working with some of the largest financial institutions in the world. He is currently the Director of Business Development and Account Management at Levvel.

Prior to joining the corporate landscape, Fred spent time in the U.S. Navy and participated in BUD/S. He also explored theater, worked as a radio DJ, and spent time in residential real estate.

John and Fred continue discussing client management in their podcast, *Account Management (A Tactical Guide to Success)*, which is available from PodBean, iTunes, Google Podcasts, and other podcast platforms.

Made in the USA
Middletown, DE
07 July 2021

43796444R00096